PURPOSE
IN CRISIS

Uncommon Secrets to finding and fulfilling
purpose in times of adversity

PURPOSE
IN CRISIS

Uncommon Secrets to finding and fulfilling
purpose in times of adversity

Dr. Samuel Ekundayo | The Purpose Preacher

DEDICATION

First, this book is dedicated to the Almighty God the giver of life and purpose. I am always amazed and grateful for the gift to write. This gift has blessed my generation and I could not be more grateful.

Most importantly, I want to dedicate this book to you! I am so grateful to God that you are alive and reading this book. It does not matter whether you have just gotten out of a crisis or you're in one right now, I have prayed for you and I believe this book will help you find purpose in crisis.

I wrote this book to help you make the most of any adversity you find yourself in, and I trust God that this book will be a blessing to your life.

CONTENTS

ACKNOWLEDGMENTS

I have to acknowledge God for the idea He gave me to write this book. In the midst of the Corona virus crisis, God said to me, 'Crisis is a call to leadership' and this inspired the idea to write this book. I am grateful I obeyed.

I am also grateful to God for my beautiful and amazing wife, Dr Blessing Oluwamayowa Ekundayo – My Dudushewa and Treasure, for believing in me and supporting me on this book as she has done for the other books I have written. I am so blessed to have you and thank you for being my helpmeet and support on this journey of purpose.

I also want to thank my parents; Pastor (Dr) John & Mary Ekundayo and parents-in-law, Rev (Dr) Ezekiel & Prof Esther Agbaje for their constant faith in me and their relentless encouragement to see me maximise my potentials. It's a blessing to have parents who believe in you.

I am grateful to everyone who has helped me with this book including my editor and friend, Pastor Sam Adetiran, who helped me to edit and format the manuscript, Opeoluwa Adebakin, who designed the beautiful cover, and Pastor Isaac Oyedepo for writing the foreword. You are all a blessing to my life and without you, I will not be where I am today. Thank you so much.

FOREWORD

God is an artist.

You were created on purpose, for a purpose, and to fulfil a purpose.

At the time of writing the foreword to this highly inspiring and timely volume, the entire world is at a standstill as we face, what some refer to as, the greatest global pandemic in a generation.

Those who were not infected were surely affected by the Corona virus (COVID-19). This makes this book, Purpose in Crisis, the book of this season, and several seasons ahead.

Life is broken into times and seasons. The days, months, and years on a calendar are what constitute the times and seasons. There is always a purpose for every time and every season.

Ecclesiastes 3:1 (King James Version) - To everything there is a season, and a time to every purpose under the heaven

Ecclesiastes 3:1 (Message Translation) - There's an opportune time to do things, a right time for everything on the earth

This book shows you how to navigate through life in every time and season that you may find yourself. Dr Samuel Ekundayo, the purpose preacher, in one of the golden chapters of this book, reveals graphically the opportunities in adversity. Adversity can end up to your advantage if only you can discover the hidden opportunities in it.

At the end of it all, a life left to chance doesn't have a chance but a life lived on purpose is a fulfilled life. God is an artist. He created, wired, and configured you for such a time as this. This isn't just another book to own. This is a masterpiece that will help you uncover, discover, and recover purpose.

There is purpose in crisis.

Isaac Oyedepo

Winners Chapel International, Maryland.

INTRODUCTION

The Oxford Learners Dictionary defines crisis as, 'A time of great danger, difficulty, or doubt when problems must be solved or important decisions must be made' or, 'A time when a problem, a bad situation or an illness is at its worst point'[1]. As I write this book, the world is in a crisis. Coronavirus of 2019 (COVID-19) is ravaging the world by storm. Countries are on lockdown. I live in New Zealand and for weeks now, our borders have been closed, restaurants shut down, airports deserted, busy highways are near empty, and only essential workers can go to work. The World Health Organisation referred to it as a global pandemic – 'A disease that spreads over a whole country or the whole world.' [2]

I have lived for more than 3.5 decades on earth and I have never witnessed anything like it. Historians said the world has experienced pandemics including the Flu Pandemic (1989 – 1990) which claimed the lives of one million people around the globe; the Spanish Flu (1918 – 1920) which claimed over a hundred million lives, history has it that some communities were at the brink of extinction. These are global crises. People also face crises in their individual lives daily.

---

[1] Oxford Learner's Dictionaries -
https://www.oxfordlearnersdictionaries.com/definition/english/crisis_1
[2] Oxford Learner's Dictionaries -
https://www.oxfordlearnersdictionaries.com/definition/english/pandemic_1

Purpose in Crisis | Samuel Ekundayo

It appears that a crisis is common to every man. Almost everyone has faced or will face a crisis in their lifetime. You have either just gone through one, you are probably going through one right now, or one is ahead of you. No matter how positive you are, you cannot escape a crisis. Crises in individual lives can come in the form of divorce, loss of a loved one, job loss, financial crisis, or a troublesome child or spouse. Some communities also experience crises in the form of terrorism, natural disasters, or wars. No matter the nature of the crises, they have one thing in common, they are unpalatable situations that are beyond human control, and because we cannot control them, they stress us and we don't like them. As a result, they put us in a form of anxiety, fear, or doubt.

WHAT CRISIS MEANS

A crisis is a change! Everyone likes change but not everyone wants to change. Whether we like it or not, change is the only constant thing. So, we cannot do anything against change. It has to happen. The world has been designed by God to make sure change is a given. I believe crisis, as with any change, was designed to grow us. God creates or allows change so that we can improve.

"God creates or allows change so that we can improve."

Crisis foster growth and improvement. No one grows in comfortable times. We only grow in difficult times. This is why a crisis is needed for us to be shaken up. When you look at cities that have suffered some type of natural disasters or terrorism, you notice a shaking that comes to improve the city. People are more united, sober, and tend to take life more seriously.

Without crisis or change many times, we humans have the tendency to cast off restraints, live life anyhow, and fail to value the essential things of life. A crisis has a way of reminding us about how short our lives are and why it is important to cherish all that we've been given. A crisis reminds us we will not live forever and every second of our lives count. A crisis offers us a fresh perspective on life.

History is an account of men and women who thrived in crisis. The truth is, champions are people who overcame something. We are only known by the things we overcame. When someone battles with cancer and they overcome it, we all celebrate them and are inspired by their story. We are inspired by people whose lives appear to have been put down as a result of a challenge or crisis but are flying.

I am reminded of a time in my life when I had a crisis. In 2006, I was an international student in Singapore and could not pay my school fees. It was about $12,000 but my parents could not afford it. By the look of things, I was going to return to Nigeria. My hopes were fading and my dreams appeared to be crumbling right before my very eyes. I remember a time I went to the immigration office to ask for more time for me to find my school fees and an immigration officer looked me in the eye and said, '*Go back to your country*!' She refused to stamp the extension that day and it appeared all hopes were dashed. I had to exit to nearby Malaysia waiting for a miracle to happen.

My parents were in church one afternoon when they met one of our church members – God bless her. She asked after me and my parents explained that I was having issues with my school fees and visa and that I have had to exit to Malaysia till it was all resolved. The woman asked my parents to see her later that week and she gave them a cheque of the entire school fees. You see, before that school fees was paid, we had cried for many nights, prayed with tears in our eyes, wondering what would become of my dream if I returned to my country. We did not know what to do, but that situation drew my family, and me closer to God. Not only did we realise that if there are people who can pray, there is a God who can answer, we also realised that tough times do not last but tough people do. We also believed in miracles again, despite the countless miracles we had seen in our lives. We saw life in a new light, we discovered God in a new way, and our dreams mattered even more.

From my story and countless others, I have come to realise that the crisis introduces us to four essential things. I will share those things with you below.

FOUR THINGS A CRISIS INTRODUCES US TO

1. Crisis Introduces or Re-introduces Us to God

The time of crisis is when people run to God. I believe God creates or allows a crisis for nations of the world to run to him. He says in His word, 'When I shut up heaven and there is no rain, or command the locusts to devour the land or send pestilence among My people. If My people who are called by My name will humble themselves, and pray and seek My face, and turn from their wicked ways, then I will hear from heaven, and will forgive their sin and heal their land'. [3] So, there are times God shuts the heavens just so that we can return to Him in repentance. There are times God will cause shaking on the earth, just so that we can turn from our wicked ways and acknowledge Him as God.

In times of crisis, God is relaying to us that He is still God. You see, we humans tend to forget this fact. We wallow in comfort and the security of our advancements and technology so much that we forget God. The more our hearts are drawn away from God as a result of the distractions we keep feeding ourselves with, the more God is not pleased with us. And because He loves us, He paves a way for us to return to Him through a crisis. Hear His words, 'The sorrows of those who run after

[3] 2 Chronicles 7:13-14 (NKJV)

another god shall multiply; their drink offerings of blood I will not pour out or take their names on my lips'.[4] It is a dangerous thing to fall into the hands of God.

Apart from the fact that crisis tells us God is still God, it also tells us we are still men. We are clay and only the breath of our nostrils holds the key to our lives. Once that breath is gone, we are dead. We cannot afford to try to compete with God or try to share His glory in any way or form. One of the reasons God often allows crisis is when we are trying to share His glory or our hearts are turned away to other gods.

During the COVID-19 pandemic, I remember one of my colleagues from our Human Resource department called me up to check on me. The whole nation was on lockdown and as lecturers, we were forced to move our teachings online. She was then tasked to give us a call to make sure we're doing well and coping under the pressure. She said, 'Samuel, how are you'? I gave her the needed account of how I was coping under the 'new normal' and when I was done, I decided to ask her the same question too. I said, 'How are you too'? She said, 'Samuel, how nice of you to ask how I am doing. My job is to check on people but now you are checking on me, thank you'.

I then asked, 'Do you believe in God'? And her response got me thinking. She said these words, 'You know what Samuel, before this crisis, I was on the fence about God. But during this crisis, I am forced to believe there is a higher power. I can see that we need a higher power

---

[4] Psalm 16:4

to save and deliver us from this crisis'. Those were are exact words. Can you see it? A crisis introduces the world to God!

During the pandemic, in the news, we saw nations of the world on their knees, bowing down, praying, singing worship songs to God, asking Him to have mercy on their countries, their families, and the world at large. The world became so united as a result. In parliaments, on the streets, in the hospitals, people were calling out to God with sober and repentant hearts. Hands raised to the sky, heads bowed and voices lifted to the heavens. It was a surreal experience.

You would agree with me that the world has turned away from God. We are so encumbered with the developments going on around us that we have allowed them to take the place of God in our lives. Gradually, we are removing God from our schools, our political systems, and communities, forgetting that God is a jealous God. See, God is merciful but He is also a consuming fire. The more we wallow in sin, the more we risk His wrath. I am reminded of the story of Sodom and Gomorrah in the Bible[5]. God had to destroy the cities because of their grave sins. The wickedness of those cities made God very angry. They were involved in all forms of immoral acts including homosexuality. When angels visited the city, their eyes of understanding had become blind so much they wanted to even rape the angels[6]. They requested for Lot, Abraham's nephew, to bring out the 'men' (who were angels) in his house out to them. They were full of many abominable things. God was

---

[5] Genesis 18 and 19
[6] Genesis 19:5

angry and ended up destroying the cities as a case study and example of what happens to people who turn away from God.

> *"Crisis reveals whose side you are."*

He brought destruction upon those cities through a massive crisis but one thing stood for sure, God saved His people before the destruction. Lot and his family were rescued. God will not destroy His children who believe in Him and are calling out to Him day and night. Crisis reveals whose side you are on. If you are on the side of God, God will protect you. But if you have your heart turned away from Him, while you still can, please return to God in repentance. He is a merciful God and He does not want you to perish. The Bible says that God is 'not willing that any should perish but that all should come to repentance.'[7] This is the heart of God because God loves the world so much that even in our grave sins, He still sent His son to die for us.

I am also reminded of the prodigal son in the scriptures[8]. A man had two sons and one day, the younger son asked for his share of inheritance from his father. He got the inheritance and ran away to another country. When he got there, he squandered everything to the point that he eventually became a destitute also because there was a great famine in the country he was in. The famine was the crisis that led him to feeding pigs and not only that, he became so starved that the pigs' food began to look attractive to him.

---

[7] 2 Peter 3:9b
[8] Luke 15:11-32

It was at that point that he finally returned to his senses. Another version of the Bible said, 'He came to Himself'. He suddenly remembered his identity and he decided to go back to his father. He said these words, 'At home, even the hired servants have enough to spare, and here I am dying of hunger. I will go home and return to my father and say, 'Father, I have sinned against both heaven and you, and I am no longer worthy of being called your son. Please take me on as a hired servant'[9]

He finally went back home and guess what? His father received him with open arms. The father saw him coming home and from afar off, filled with love and compassion, he ran towards him, embraced him, and kissed him. He apologised to his father and his father accepted him again as his son. He even asked for the finest of robes to be put on his back, a ring on his finger, and sandals for his feet. Not only that, but a party was also thrown for him. His father said these words, 'For this son of mine was dead and has now returned to life. He was lost but now found.[10] What a father! The father in that story refers to God! He is an ever-loving father. No matter how far we may have gone away from Him, He is more than happy to receive us again into His loving and compassionate arms. All we need to do, like the prodigal son, is to return to our senses and turn our hearts to Him.

Hear this, the crisis was not meant to destroy you, it was meant to bring your heart to repentance, to introduce or reintroduce you to God.

---

[9] Luke 15:17-18
[10] Luke 15:24

1. Crisis Introduces Us to Ourselves

One of the good things about a crisis is that it reveals who we truly are. If you want to know who people are, see them when everything is falling apart. Human life is reduced to bare bones when things are not going well. However, one thing is certain, the way God has created man is that He puts in us this intestinal fortitude to withstand a crisis. Even in crisis, with God on our side, we can overcome.

> *"If you want to know who people are, see them when everything is falling apart."*

Overcoming in crisis requires digging deep. As a result, during a crisis, there tends to be an upsurge in creative problem-solving. It is during crisis and adversity that problem solvers emerge. In the current pandemic in which I am writing this book, as an academic, my colleagues and I have been forced to start teaching online. Not only have we had to think about creative ways to make sure we deliver our contents online, but we are also providing emotional and pastoral support to our students. Many of my colleagues before the crisis have blatantly argued against fully going online to teach, but the crisis has forced everyone to adapt and I tell you, while it's challenging, we are making it work.

Due to my love for Psychology research, I did some study to find out why this is the case and I found the reasons why creativity and problem-solving takes an upsurge in times of adversity as follows:

People often choose tasks with shorter deadlines over the ones with longer deadlines even if the latter offers higher rewards because the former is viewed as relatively uncomplicated. A crisis forces our tasks into shorter deadlines and as a result, we tend to be found working tirelessly towards a solution.

In adversity, people are always forced to ask, 'What do I know that can help in this crisis'? 'What skills do I have'? All of a sudden, there is a consciousness of the knowledge you have, your past experiences, the people you know, skills you have acquired, and heuristics that can be applied to the problem.

An imminent threat forces the human mind to act in defence. Psychologists have found that imminent threats tend to energise us and get us focused. We tend to get more physical energy as part of our flight, flight, or freeze response. Sometimes, fear makes us channel that energy into negative things such as worry, anxiety, depression, or a feeling of helplessness. However, we can be resolute in the face of adversity to channel that energy into a fight response such as 'fighting with our brain, technical skills, and emotional skills'.[11]

Also, when our habits are disrupted, humans tend to gain a spark of creativity to re-evaluate their old ways of doing things and as a result, create a new way of doing what has to be done. And such evaluations often come with realisations of some of the redundant, ineffective ways we have been doing things before the crisis. As a result, we can use new tools, methods, and techniques we may not have considered if not for the crisis.

---

[11] Source: https://www.psychologytoday.com/us/blog/in-practice/202003/why-are-people-more-creative-in-crisis

A crisis tends to bring novel problems to the surface. When we are faced with a problem we have not needed to solve before, we are forced into thinking and acting creatively. Novel problems will most likely require novel solutions or a new way of applying existing solutions. Even our familiar resources gain new uses and the things we never thought useful suddenly become valuable. During the COVID-19 pandemic, web conference tools like ZOOM became very prominent. The company's shares surged to a record high in the market overtaking some renowned brands. The main reason was that the pandemic caused a user base surge of 2,900%.[12] People were forced to hold work meetings, church meetings, conferences, webinars, and training on the platform as nations were on lockdown and people were not allowed to gather.

In essence, it is in the downtimes of our lives that we are most creative. We do not suddenly become creative, we had it in us but the crisis allowed them to emerge either to help us survive or thrive.

Many human developments have emerged for this very reason, from the Stone Age to the modern world we now live in.

2. Crisis Introduces Us to Others

One of the things a crisis does is to force us to seek help. If you are in a crisis in your life, please don't try to go through it alone. A time of crisis is a kind of lonely time but loneliness is a choice. You can choose to get the help you need. I wrote in my book, 30 Reasons to Stay, the importance of seeking help in times of adversity. The very reason many

---

[12] https://markets.businessinsider.com/news/stocks/zoom-stock-price-surges-following-nasdaq-inclusion-coronavirus-video-conference-2020-4-1029127632

people contemplate suicide or become clinically depressed is that they are trying to deal with their issues alone. You don't have to go through times of adversity alone. Churches, health centres, community help centres, are places you can find help. A crisis is your opportunity to be introduced to others who can be of help.

"It is in the downtimes of our lives that we are most creative."

"A crisis is your opportunity to be introduced to others who can be of help."

Also, in times of crisis, we are often introduced to the real nature of others around us. All of a sudden, the characters, attributes, attitudes, and aptitudes of the people around you become noticeable. I am reminded of the words of John Churton Collins who said, 'In prosperity, our friends know us, in adversity, we know our friends'. Aren't those words so true? Anyone can and would love to be your friend in times of prosperity, but as soon as you are going through a valley-like situation, they disappear and are nowhere to be found.

Success has many fathers, while failure is an orphan. Not many people want to be associated with you when things are not going well for you. The very people that have dined with you when things were going good will desert you when you are in crisis. Listen, this is normal. I know this can be quite discouraging but don't let that affect you too much. It's a human tendency to relate with you this way, but guess what? Some true friends stick closer (than your siblings) – those who will stick with you no matter how hot the furnace is.

Purpose in Crisis | Samuel Ekundayo

I remember a time of crisis in my life. I was in New Zealand as an international student for my Ph.D. I had started the Ph.D. study with so much joy and enthusiasm. My primary supervisor treated me well and all was going well. All of a sudden in the middle of my programme, my supervisors started to complain that I was not doing enough and my progress was poor and below the standards expected of a Ph.D. student. It was one of the down moments of my life. I would cry almost every day in my room alone.

My fellow Ph.D. students appeared to just leave me to myself, even the people I had helped with some of their works and reports. It was as though they had no idea what was going on, but I had a friend who stood by me. Ammar (from Pakistan) would always encourage me. I also had a roommate then who was also a Ph.D. student who knew all I was going through. He would tell me about how he had been through the same thing and got his breakthrough in the end. He would inspire and encourage me to keep going on. He was right, the crisis was just for a season. Thank God for friends like that.

So, if you are in a crisis, stay close to those friends who genuinely love you and want the best for you. They will always be there for you. Don't cast them away thinking you have to go through it alone, that would be dangerous. See, evil and darkness thrive in isolation. When you isolate yourself, things are only going to get worse, but when you find the right friends, people you can lean on, you will find the burden quite easier to bear.

When Jesus was on his way to the cross, the soldiers were flogging him, blood was gushing out from all parts of his body, but his disciples had disappeared and deserted Him. Many of those close to Jesus at that time did not want to be seen with Him so that they don't share in Jesus' death or get crucified with Him. But records have it that there was a man from Cyrene named Simon[13], who was just passing by on that day, who helped Jesus carry the cross. What a legacy! He showed us what true friends should do when a friend is in crisis. I mean, Jesus was condemned to crucifixion, yet a foreigner decided he was going to be of help.

If you are reading this, always remember Simon from Cyrene and be the help your friends need in times of crisis. It is one thing for others to be there for you in your times of crisis, but you can also be there for others too in their time of crisis. The way life was designed is such that no one is immune to crisis. If you are doing well today, it's a season. There would come a season you may not be doing well. It's not a curse. Be the shoulder someone can cry on today. Be the person others can lean on today because no one knows tomorrow.

Another reason people desert us in times of crisis is if we have deserted them before in their downtimes too. Listen, 'A man who has friends must himself be friendly but there is a friend who sticks closer than a brother.' [14] If you have not been there for anyone, if you have not shown yourself as a true friend when others are going through tough times, don't be expecting them to stick close to you when you are going through yours. There is a likelihood they will treat you the very same way you have treated them. That scripture is very clear, if you want

---

[13] Mark 15:21, Matthew 27:32, Luke 23:26
[14] Proverbs 18:24 NKJV

friends, then you have to be friendly as well. You have to be there for people if you want them to be there for you.

Another perspective is that a crisis fosters partnership and collaboration with others. It's one thing to receive help from people or for them to be the shoulders you cry on, but it's another thing to enter into partnerships that will change your life post-crisis. I have heard about many people who lost their jobs and started a business with a friend that eventually thrived. The crisis you are in could be an opportunity to collaborate or partner with someone on a venture that will be life-changing or life-defining. Don't miss that opportunity.

In the era of the COVID-19 I wrote this book in, I had the privilege of being introduced to great men and women from all over the world. People I ordinarily would not have easily been able to meet or collaborate with, the crisis provided that platform and leverage, and boy, I maximised it! I took advantage of it. You too can do the same.

3. Crisis Introduces Us to Opportunities

The Oxford Learner's Dictionaries defines opportunity as 'A time when a particular situation makes it possible to do or achieve something'[15]. I believe a crisis is that time or situation you can achieve a lot. I am sure you read that and in your mind, you're like 'Dr Samuel, what do you mean?' See, the crisis was not designed to destroy you, it was meant to introduce you to the problems you can solve, problems you are to proffer solutions to. Psychologists have found out that if we do not

---

[15] Source:
https://www.oxfordlearnersdictionaries.com/definition/english/opportunity_1

allow our negative emotions such as fear and doubts to take over our minds, crisis and adversity are actually the time our creativity is at the highest.

At the time of writing this book (the year 2020), the two words I am running with are flexibility and creativity. I got these two words when I attended John Maxwell's Leadership seminar organised by LeadUK earlier in the year. Creativity means there is a solution to every problem, and flexibility means there is more than one solution to every problem. No matter how dark, gloomy, tough, life-threatening, or hopeless your situation appears, there is a solution. Not only that, but there is also more than one solution.

It is a matter of perspective. Wayne Dyer says it like this, 'If you change the way you look at things, the things you look at change.' This means our problems are often a reflection or result of our perspectives. This is why fear is bondage. If your perspective is fuelled by fear, you will see wrongly. But if you are full of faith, you will see things rightly. This is why I am a person of faith and I enjoy looking at things from God's perspective.

Let me share one thing I discovered from my many years of studying the Word of God. This will bless and inspire you. Do you know every single time people had problems in the Bible and they complained to God (in the Old Testament) or Jesus (in the New Testament), there was never a time that God sympathised with them? There was a time in my secret place that I had to ask God, 'You are the God that said, "For we do not have a high priest who is unable to empathize with our weaknesses, but we have one who has been tempted in every way, just as we are yet he did not sin"[16], so how come You don't sympathise with us in our pains'? The reply I got shocked me. God said, 'I feel your pains but my goal is for you to realise pain is inevitable but suffering is a choice.' Wow! This is why God always snapped people away from their pain so they can let go of their suffering and start seeing things from a new perspective.

> *"There are opportunities in every crisis, it's only a matter of our perspective."*

There was a time Jesus visited his friends, Mary and Martha, when their brother, Lazarus died. Before Lazarus died, they sent a message to Jesus that Lazarus was sick. They even told him, 'Jesus, he whom you love is sick.'[17] It's very clear Jesus loved Lazarus but his response was not that of sympathy but that of a switch in perspective. He said, 'This sickness is not unto death, but for the glory of God, that the Son of God may be glorified through it.' Can you believe that? Would you not have expected Him to say something like, 'Oh, so sorry to hear that. I will be on my way shortly?' Instead, Jesus offers a fresh perspective, that the pain is temporary and that even in that pain, God wants to reveal His glory. Isn't that amazing?

> *"There are opportunities in every crisis, it's only a matter of our perspective. "*

By the time Lazarus eventually died, Mary and Martha were almost trying to blame Jesus. They said, 'If you had been here (when we sent

---

[16] Hebrews 4:15 (NIV)
[17] John 11:3

18

you the message while he was still sick), my brother would not have died.'[18] (Emphasis added) Jesus' response is worth studying. He said, 'Where have you laid him'? He offered a new perspective again. By the time Jesus got to the tomb, He wept but that did not last long because He saw the opportunity to glorify God in the crisis. There are opportunities in every crisis, it's only a matter of our perspective.

Jesus said, 'Did I not say to you that if you would believe, you would see the glory of God?'[19] That statement is worth meditating on for days! You see, when you look around you at a time of crisis, what you see can prevent you from seeing opportunities for God to be glorified even in that crisis, but when you choose not to look with your eyes but instead believe, you will see the incredible opportunities awaiting you. Jesus understood this and taught us this great lesson – pay attention to your belief, your faith, and that will change what you see.

We should be more affected by what we believe than what we see. This is why people of faith do not let what they see to affect their belief, instead, they control what they see by their belief. Successful people do not move by what they see, they are moved by their faith. No wonder the Bible says, 'For we walk by faith, not by sight.'[20] Another place says, 'The just shall live by faith.'[21] Why is this very important? It is key because what you see is temporary! 'So we don't look at the troubles we can see now; rather, we fix our gaze on things that cannot be seen. For

---

[18] John 11:32
[19] John 11:40
[20] 2 Corinthians 5:7 (KJV)
[21] Hebrews 10:38

the things we see now will soon be gone, but the things we cannot see will last forever.'[22]

What you can see will soon be gone but what you cannot see (a function of your faith) will last forever. Opportunities in adversity lie in the things the ordinary eyes cannot see. In fact, what is happening on your inside is more important than what is happening around you during a crisis. Psychologists talk about the locus of control. They advise that successful people are controlled by their internal locus of control whereas other people are controlled by an external locus of control. People with an internal locus of control tend to have control over their situations and circumstances. They do not give up easily. They can be strong in the face of difficulties. Not only that, but they can also discern the opportunity in difficulty. William Shakespeare must be one of them because he said and I quote, 'Sweet are the uses of adversity.' What a perspective!

I wrote this book in the season of the COVID-19 virus that took the entire world by storm. While economies are crashing, businesses are shutting down, people are losing their jobs; some organisations are thriving. ZOOM Inc. stocks rose to a record high, Amazon had to recruit more staff to handle their orders, Netflix had to invest more in their platform to give people an expanded and fun experience while they are at home during the lockdown. It's a matter of perspective.

My friend, Pastor Isaac Oyedepo, said, 'Crisis can either punish you or polish you.' If you fail to see opportunities in adversity, it will punish

---

[22] 2 Corinthians 4:18

you, but if you would lay hold of the opportunities therein, it will polish you and you will come out as pure and valuable gold in the end. A crisis is a time to look for opportunities to arise and shine. 'Arise, shine; for your light has come! And the glory of the Lord is risen upon you. For behold, the darkness shall cover the earth, and deep darkness the people; but the Lord will arise over you, and His glory will be seen upon you.'[23] Did you notice it says that darkness shall cover the earth and deep darkness the people? But did you also notice it continued by saying that the Lord will arise over you and His glory will be seen upon you? That's the same perspective Jesus had earlier.

Anytime there is a crisis and everything looks dark and bleak, it is an opportunity for the glory of God to be seen upon you. Don't deny God the expression of His glory in and through you by having a wrong perspective in crisis.

In this season of the COVID-19 as I write this book, I have leveraged incredible opportunities I was able to see through the eyes of faith. I went bold launching courses that sold way more than they did before the crisis. I started a 30-day Boot camp for writers that has now become a major part of my business. For the first launch, 13 people signed up and they had a life-transforming experience writing their books. Some had the books in them for years, but the Boot camp was the opportunity to get it out. I also launched my coaching programme on a grand scale and I got more one-on-one (premium) sign-ups than I ever did before the crisis. It was an incredible opportunity because I leveraged the season of crisis. I saw the waves were going technocentric and I took

---

[23] Isaiah 60:1-2 (NKJV)

advantage of the waves. Rather than sulk, weep, and cry, I saw the opportunity and advantages and I took them.

1

What Is Purpose?

DEFINITION OF PURPOSE

Everything exists for a reason! There is nothing created without a purpose. This is why when the purpose of a thing is not known, it can be abused. Someone said, 'The purpose of life is to live a life of purpose.' When God wanted to create man, He had thought about it long and hard and then made a declaration – 'Let us make man, in our own image, in our own likeness.'[24] He didn't just make the man because He was bored. He made man intentionally.

This reminds me of an analogy I heard some time back – God is an artist. Every artist creates things twice; first in their minds and then in reality. I heard about how Michelangelo would walk around a particular piece of wood or stone for days just contemplating, thinking, and ruminating about what he would sculpt out of it. Days of creating the masterpiece of sculpture in his mind before ever grabbing a chisel. Similarly, you are God's masterpiece, and He carefully thought about you way before your father and mother met. He was intentional about the combination of traits, genes, and temperament required for you to fulfil the purpose He was creating you for. This is worth getting excited about. The day I made this discovery, I nearly hit the roof. Isn't it

---

[24] Genesis 1:26

amazing to realise I am a major part of God's plan for His kingdom on earth? There is something God wants to do in the world that you're needed for! I love how the late Dr. Myles Munroe puts it, 'Your existence is evidence that this generation needs something that your life contains'

> *"Your sense of significance, worth, and fulfilment is embedded in the discovery of your purpose."*

So, God thought to Himself, I need an extension of myself on earth - humans that carry my nature, my likeness, my glory to nurture and care for the earth. The heart of God and His purpose was made clear when He created everything but delayed sending rain because Man was not yet created.[25] This is why I believe no man or anything created for that matter exists without a reason.

No man is a mistake. No man is an experiment. No man is a product of 'natural selection'. God carefully and thoughtfully formed you because of a specific purpose He wants to achieve with you on the surface of the earth. This is why you must know the heart of God about your creation. The day you get an insight into your WHY, your life will take a completely new turn. Your sense of significance, worth, and fulfilment is embedded in the discovery of your purpose.

It is dangerous to be alive and not know why. If you do not know why you are alive, you will struggle. You will only be surviving instead of thriving. You will live your entire life in the rat race when you're supposed to dominate and rule. God has designed you the way you are

---

[25] Genesis 2:7

so that fulfilling your purpose becomes very natural to you. This means anything you do outside of the purpose of God for your life will frustrate you.

It will be a futile effort trying to change who you are. This is the source of depression, anxiety, and emptiness for many people in our world right now. They are constantly trying to change themselves. The best way to live life is to accept you and flow with your purpose.

So, your purpose is God's original intent for creating you. This knowledge alone can set you free from trying to compete with others or trying to be who you were not made to be. However, there are a few more things you need to know about your purpose so you can be confident in times of crisis.

FIVE THINGS YOU MUST KNOW ABOUT YOUR PURPOSE (CONCERNING A CRISIS)

#1 – Purpose Cannot Be Destroyed

No man, no devil, no crisis, can destroy your purpose. I don't care the kind of crisis that has befallen you or affecting the world right now, one thing you must always remember is that nothing can destroy God's purpose for your life, not even your failures. As long as you are alive you can still fulfil your purpose.

"As long as you are alive you can still fulfil your purpose."

Sometimes in our failures, we become so guilty and reproached to the point we feel like we have reached a point that our purpose can't be salvaged. Listen, there is no point in life where your purpose is destroyed. I remember this particular common analogy. If you crush under your feet a hundred dollar note or squeeze it to the point it's almost unrecognisable; does that change its value? No, it doesn't. It's still a hundred dollars. Only death can end a purpose that has not seen the light of day, but a purpose that is already active cannot even be put out by death. This is why people who live their lives fulfilling purpose still appear to be living and their works still impacting lives long after they are dead and gone. This is because death has no power over purpose!

"You are a carrier of light for a specific darkness in our world."

#2 – Purpose Is A Solution to A Problem

Your purpose was given for the benefit of humanity. You are a carrier of light for a specific darkness in our world. In other words, you are an authentic and unique solution to a problem that exists in the world. God has put some abilities, capabilities, specific natural gifts, and talents in you to proffer solutions to some problems the way only you can! This is why until you show up, some problems may linger. This is why I am convinced you are sitting on a gold mine if you are failing to realise the solution you carry.

Remember where we started from, God did not create anything because He was bored. You were born because there is a problem in the world that you have been uniquely crafted to address. And that's why even though I encourage people to find their purpose, I also believe purpose also finds us because there are issues, problems that keep calling out your name. When you look left and right, it's like they are the only problems that are so vivid to you in the world, it means purpose is calling out your name. You owe the world what you carry! Your purpose is a solution! Yes, a solution to a specific problem!

#3 – Purpose Is God's Expression through You

Whenever you fulfil your purpose, it is God expressing Himself through you. This is why the fulfilment of purpose is not about you, it's about what God is doing through you. How do I know this? When God created you, He breathed into your nostrils the breath of life [26] – meaning He imparted Himself into you and more like saying 'Everything you do expresses your authentic self, I am revealed in you.' The word for breath is transliterated '*nasham*' in the original Hebrew the Bible was written in, which means 'Divine inspiration.' This is why the entire opposite of purpose is trying to be someone you are not. Whenever you are trying to be someone you are not, you are denying yourself the expression of God through you.

> *"Whenever you are trying to be someone you are not, you are denying yourself the expression of God through you."*

There are many people in our world doing all they can to be someone else, talk like someone else, dress like someone else other themselves; as a result, they are not functioning or operating their authentic selves and this is dangerous. Living this way is also denying the world of your true

---

[26] Genesis 2:7

and authentic self. What you carry is unique and powerful. It's fulfilling and beautiful when you share it with the world.

#4 – Purpose Is Giving Responsibility to Your Ability

There are abilities that God has given you but the only way those abilities will produce fruits is when you give them responsibility. The powerful thing about your abilities is that they are seeds. If you fail to put them to work, they die because anything you fail to use, you lose. Only what you use can bring you value. So, when you give responsibility to your abilities, you grow in value.

Your purpose is the source of your value. Your gifts were given to you to help you fulfil your purpose. Just like function was built into anything created for it to fulfil its purpose, you were designed the way you function as you've been built to function. God does not waste resources. Every ability, all that you know how to do and have a passion for were intentional. Whatever God has put in you, He put there for a reason.

"Your purpose is the source of your value."

#5 – Purpose Is An Assignment

One of life's greatest discovery is to realise you came here on an assignment. Yes, your purpose is your life's assignment. As an academic, it's imperative to let you know that I know about assignments very well. Let me share with you an experience I had sometime back on my journey as a lecturer. I had this student (let's call him Henry) who was older than me by more than a decade. Henry was a student on one of my courses that had several assignments in the initial weeks of the course. Every time I hand them the instructions for each assignment, Henry had one thing or the other to say. He would argue with me on why he thinks I did not give the right instructions in the assignment. He would go away and do it his way and how he deemed right completely ignoring my instructions.

> *"Your purpose is an assignment with specific instructions you must adhere to."*

Of course, I always gave him a zero! The next week, when I hand in another assignment, he would argue again and go away to do what he thought was right. When the results came out, he would see a zero because he did something completely out of line with what he'd been asked to do. I think about the fourth week, Henry came to meet me in my office and said these exact words, 'Hi Samuel, I don't think I should be arguing with my lecturer about his assignment, right'? 'I don't think so too', I responded. Since then, Henry stopped arguing with me and he did the assignments according to the instructions given and he got his full marks.

See life just the same way. Our purpose is our assignment and God is the lecturer. Every time you think you can do the opposite of what you have been designed to do, you are behaving like Henry – you're arguing with your lecturer. You will never get anything but zero! You will keep failing and getting frustrated until you come back to your senses, like Henry, to realise you're not supposed to be arguing with your lecturer, the giver of the assignment.

Purpose in Crisis | **Samuel Ekundayo**

Your purpose is an assignment with specific instructions you must adhere to. If you look into our world right now, you will find many people arguing with their Maker and Creator about their life's assignment. As such, they live life frustrated, empty, and unfulfilled. This reminds me of one of my favourite scriptures – 'A person may have many ideas concerning God's plan for his life, but only the designs of His (God's) purpose will succeed in the end.'[27] This means that it is natural for you to want to argue with God's plans for your life, but it will lead to frustration because only God's purpose for your life will bring you success.

---

[27] Proverbs 19:21 TPT

2

A Call To Leadership

Early into the year 2020, I was in the United Kingdom attending a John Maxwell conference when I heard this statement in my spirit, 'I need you to unlearn and re-learn Leadership.' I knew it was God speaking to me. You see, before that word dropped in my spirit, I held some leadership positions in church and my community. I did not know why God told me that and I did not ask but I just decided to obey. In fact, at the conference, I straight away bought three leadership books – Leadershift, Developing The Leader Within You 2.0 (both by John Maxwell) and Becoming a Leader (by the Late Dr. Myles Munroe). While in my hotel room in the UK, I started feasting on 'Becoming a Leader'. It was amazing some of the things I started to learn.

I returned from the United Kingdom and my boss at work called me to tell me she was contemplating promoting me to Programme Leader as the colleague of mine occupying the position had talked about stepping down to take on a bigger project. I said to myself, 'This must be the reason God asked me to unlearn and re-learn leadership.' I said that because the role required that I manage staff, something quite new for me in my role as a lecturer. It would be my first call to management in my career as an academic. I was excited.

"Crisis is a call to leadership"

A month after, the COVID-19 pandemic shook the world and the entire world was on lockdown. The World Health Organisation (W.H.O) declared the virus a pandemic and the crisis took the world by storm. People were dying every day in the nations of the world. The news of the crisis alone caused panic, doubt, and uncertainty in the hearts of people. Leaders were affected, businesses had to close down, and economies suffered. Amid the crisis, one morning, I heard God say to me, 'Crisis is a call to leadership.' When I heard that statement, I wrote it down and as soon as I did, I got the idea of this book. I knew God wanted me to write about it, so I continued to do some study. In my study, I found evidence both in the bible and in history.

BIBLICAL EXAMPLES

A crisis raises leaders. It is in a crisis that voices are heard. In fact, from time immemorial, permit me to say it like this, God uses a crisis to raise a voice – a voice of leadership. I am reminded of some biblical voices that were raised as a result of a crisis. When you read about these people, you would realise that a crisis is an opportunity for your voice to be heard.

Esther – The Queen

One of the examples of voices God raised in a time of crisis was Queen Esther. Esther was a slave in a foreign land. She was being raised by her uncle, Mordecai. She suddenly found herself in the palace as queen because the former queen misbehaved and the king decided to look for another. Esther's beauty and attitude caught the eye of the queen so much he did not even bother to find out about her background until he had betrothed her, I believe.

And then a crisis happened! The king's second in command, Haman, decided he was going to wipe out the Jews in the land, of which Esther was one. He hated Mordecai with strong passion because he would not bow and pay homage to him. The king promoted Haman, making him the most powerful official in the kingdom. Everyone in the kingdom, including the king's officials, was expected to bow to and pay homage to Haman.

Haman was angry that Mordecai refused to bow to him and show him respect day after day. As a result, he decided to wipe out every Jew in the kingdom. He started his plot by deceiving the king into signing a decree to kill all the Jews. The decree was written exactly as Haman wanted it and the king signed it. Haman joyfully moved his plot into full gear, setting up how he would kill all the Jews – young, old, men, women, and children – in one single day.

When Mordecai heard about it, he tore his clothes trying to get the attention of the king. When he could not get access to the king, he sent a message to Esther that reads, 'If you keep quiet at a time like this, deliverance and relief for the Jews will arise from some other place, but you and your relatives will die. Who knows if perhaps you were made queen for just such a time as this'?[28]

---

[28] Esther 4:14 NLT

We need to dissect Mordecai's words as there are some important points for us to consider in it. The first: If you keep quiet at a time like this, deliverance and relief for the Jews will arise from some other place… This statement can also be divided into two parts. So, let's call this first part 1a.

If you keep quiet at a time like this

I feel that scripture is letting us know that the time of crisis is not a time to keep quiet. It's not a time to be silent. It's time for your voice to be heard. It's time to do something. It's time to act. Too many people keep quiet in times of adversity and they just let it run them over. One of the reasons for this quietness, as we can see in the case of Esther, is comfort. You see, one of the most dangerous things in life is comfort. Someone said, 'The enemy of success is not failure, it's comfort.' When you are too comfortable, you don't speak when your voice is required. When you are too comfortable, you fail to act when doing something is what is required of you.

Mordecai had to remind Esther – 'Don't think because you are now comfortable in the palace, this problem is not your concern. Don't you dare keep quiet at this time, because if you do, the disaster will reach you too, it's only a matter of time.' That's the way I can paraphrase Mordecai's message. You see, it's not a threat, but a reminder to Esther about her identity. Comfort sometimes makes us forget or lose our identity. Some people even forget their purpose once they get comfortable.

I believe this is why a crisis is necessary. A crisis is necessary to shake us up. A crisis is required to get us uncomfortable. We only grow when things are not comfortable. Our creativity is visible when we are uncomfortable. In fact, throughout history, advancements are made through crises, wars, droughts, and famine. Crisis teaches us to be a voice! During a crisis is a time for our voices to be heard. We must be the beacon of hope, faith, love, and peace the world needs during a crisis.

> *"A crisis causes a stirring within you to act and when you do, there is a likelihood purpose will find you."*

I believe purpose finds us in crisis when we find or lend our voice in it. I am going to say that again in a way that you would understand. A crisis causes a stirring within you to act and when you do, there is a likelihood purpose will find you. Another reason some are silent is because of fear. Esther may also have been hesitant because she was afraid. She may have been afraid that eventually, the king would find out she was a Jew. And the outcome of that finding may terrify her, but thank God for mentors. Mordecai was able to charge her up and remind her of her identity. As soon as she read from Mordecai, her mind was made. She decided she was no longer going to be silent. This leads me to part 1b.

Deliverance and relief for the Jews will arise from some other place

If you fail to be the voice of hope, faith, love, and peace in a time of difficulty, God will raise other people. One of the most dangerous things in life is to be given the ability yet to fail to be responsible. A crisis is your call to give responsibility to your ability. Your purpose is to give responsibility to your abilities. Until your abilities meet with responsibility, you will be as good as having no ability.

Esther was in the palace, with the king, yet until Mordecai's letter to her, she was looking for all kinds of excuses. Maybe you are reading this and you are situated in a season of crisis and you are failing to give responsibility to your abilities because of one reason or the other, you are treading on dangerous grounds. The latter part of that statement said, '…but you and your relatives will die.' It was a reminder to Esther that sounded like this, 'If you fail to give your abilities responsibility, you will not be exempted from disaster.' However, should you act, rise to the call, you are not just going to survive, you will thrive.

The second part of that scripture poses a question:

Who knows if perhaps you were made queen for just such a time as this?

You are reading this and you are in a season of crisis. Could it be that you were born or made for such a time as this? Have you ever thought of or asked yourself this question? So many people just panic in the face of crises and problems and do not bother to ask themselves this critical question. Mordecai's question caused a shift in the mind of Esther.

William Arthur Ward said, 'Adversity causes some men to break, others to break records.' The Bible says, 'If you fail in the days of adversity, your strength is small.'[29] The Hebrew word for "strength" is

---

[29] Proverbs 24:10

transliterated as "*koach*" which means ability! Your ability is too small if you fail in the days of a crisis. This is why it is important to develop and refine your abilities way before a crisis arrives. We prepare for war in times of peace, not during the war. When you refine your abilities before the crisis, you will find that you will thrive and not just survive during the crisis.

Thank God Esther had developed her faith in God, her ability, and her attitude before the crisis. No wonder she was no longer afraid. She requested that the Jews in the land fast and pray for three days and made up her mind to go and see the king. See, going to see the king at the time, even though you are a queen was against the laws of the land. You only got to the king when he sends for you. But you could see the resolve, the ability, the power, the strength in Esther's words. She said, 'Though it is against the law, I will go in to see the king. If I must die, I must die.'[30] Another version says it like this, 'If I perish, I perish.' That statement could only have come from someone whose strength in a season of crisis is not little. She meant, 'I will do something about this. I will give responsibility to my ability. I will not be silent. I will rise. I will be a beacon of hope, love, faith, and peace at this time.' And God helped her. She did it!

She went into the king, the king received her and granted her request for the Jews not to be killed. Not only that, the king also rewarded Mordecai for saving his life and promoted him in the place of Haman.

David – The Shepherd Boy

---

[30] Esther 4:16c (NLT)

Purpose in Crisis | **Samuel Ekundayo**

Another example in the Bible was David. You see, David was the youngest son of his parents, but he had a controversial birth. Some Bible commentaries talk about how his birth was not one his parents were proud of. As a result, they left him with the task of shepherding his father's sheep, hoping a wild animal would kill him. They saw him as a reproach to the family. He would not even eat with the family, according to some Bible scholars, to the point that even when the prophet Samuel was going to anoint one of Jesse (David's father) sons as king, David was not counted worthy to be there, until Samuel had to later send for him. David was anointed to be the replacement for king Saul who was still on the throne at the time. But this is not really what I want to bring out from the story of David.

A season of crisis befell the Israelites at a point. There was a Philistine giant, Goliath by name. He was a champion. He was nine feet tall and had a presence that scared not just the common man but the entire army of Israel. He challenged every single one of them and no one dared to face him or talk back at him. He reproached and held the entire nation to ransom for forty days, every morning and evening. The Bible recorded that after his boastful and reproaching words to the Israelites, Saul and the Israelites would become 'terrified and deeply shaken' to their bones.

David's brothers were part of the army and they were part of those shaken to the bones by Goliath's threats. Like the rest of the army of Israel, David's brothers too could do nothing but fear. One morning, David's father thought it wise to send David to the battlefield with a basket of food for his brothers. He was instructed to deliver the basket and come back with a report of what was going on there. David left the sheep he was looking after for another shepherd to answer his father's call.

"If you have developed yourself and refined your gifts for purpose way before the crisis arrives, you will never be afraid of crisis."

By the time he got to the battleground, he noticed what was going on. He was able to witness Goliath's threats for that day. He also saw how the Israelites took to their heels in fright as soon as Goliath showed up. Word got to David about how Goliath had been doing the same thing for forty days. It was as if David was excited by the crisis, such that he asked, 'Please, what will a man get for killing this Philistine and ending his defiance of Israel?'[31] I mean, the only way you will be interested in the rewards for killing a man is if you are interested in going to war with the man. You need to understand here that David was not part of the army. He had no military training, but there was something peculiar about this young man.

While tendering his father's sheep, he had developed his battle skills. His Curriculum Vitae (CV) included details of killing wild beats like a lion and bear. He had lived in the wild enough that he was not surviving there but thriving. I can imagine a young man that wild beasts would have come to respect and fear. By his records of defeating those wild beasts in the wilderness, David had this confidence that none of the armies of Israel had. He was not boastful, but confident. If you have

---

[31] 1 Samuel 17:26

developed yourself and refined your gifts for purpose way before the crisis arrives, you will never be afraid of a crisis. You will be full of confidence. You will be full of faith. You will be full of hope. Other people will be scared. Others will be shaken to their teeth but your words will be full of faith. You will look unreal. The words you say will look like you are full of pride. And that was what happened.

David made sure he got his fact right about the rewards for killing Goliath. They told him, the person would get the king's daughter as a wife and the person's entire family would be exempted from paying taxes! David was like, 'this is too good to pass.' Amazing! A crisis is a call to leadership. But for you to thrive as a leader or to answer the leadership call, you need to have developed your leadership ability, way before the crisis arrives. The time of crisis is not the time to start developing those abilities. They need to have been sharpened, refined enough to help you thrive in the face of adversity.

In the words of William Shakespeare, 'Sweet are the uses of adversity.' David understood this principle and he was willing to put it to work. He refused to go back to his dad. He went straight to the king and asked to see him. He said to the King, 'Sir, don't worry about this Philistine, I'll go fight him!' Such confidence! I need you to get that David was a teenager at this point. That was why he was not in the military. By the policies of the land, he was not even supposed to feature on the battlefield because of his age. But the nation was in a crisis and the only person brave enough was a teenager.

Saul did all he could to discourage the young man, but he was too determined to be denied the opportunity he wanted. He was too passionate. By the time he started to talk about his experience of how he had killed a lion and a bear and rescued lambs from their teeth while tending his father's sheep, Saul had to oblige him. His stories were not of the feeble but the brave. His accounts were too unreal. I mean, how can a teenager talk about grabbing a lion by the jaw and clubbing it to death? Saul knew there was something extraordinary about the young man so he let him go. He even offered him his armour. David tested them and said, 'I can't go in these… I am not used to them.' He was too confident to put on anything he was not used to. Do you see the importance of giving responsibility to his abilities way before the crisis arrived? He was very clear about what he was used to. He knew what would work for him and what would not. In the face of a king, with all due respect, he declared, 'I am not used to them.'

All David took with him were five smooth stones and a sling. These were his weapon. He was used to them. You can tell he had been practising. You can tell he was consistent with those. I remember reading Malcolm Gladwell's book, David and Goliath. In the book, he talked about how many of us often think David was the underdog in the battle against Goliath. He felt David had the upper hand when you look at his weapon and the size of Goliath. With his weapon, Goliath was too big to miss. Malcolm made it clear that the nature of the weapon was such that David had the intention and expectation of hitting Goliath at his most vulnerable spot, which was between his eyes. And, boy, did he get it?

Before I get to the end of the story, I need to tell you about the level of confidence David exuded when he finally left the king's palace and faced Goliath face to face. Goliath had some derogatory words to offer to David but guess what? David was used to those kinds of words. Even his family despised him so he had overcome the worst words. He was not moved by them. He exchanged his own words too. His words are enough to study for days! He said to Goliath, 'You come to me with sword, and javelin, but I come to you in the name of the Lord of Heaven's Armies – the God of the armies of Israel, whom you have defiled. Today, the Lord will conquer you, and I will kill you and cut off your head. And everyone assembled here will know that the Lord rescues His people, but not with sword and spear. This is the Lord's battle and He will give you to us.'[32] Did I hear you say, 'What effrontery'? I have taken time to study David's words and I discovered that even though David had defeated the lion and the bear in the bush, he didn't come to Goliath with the confidence of his history, but the consciousness of his God!

There is something about the consciousness of the presence of God. It assassinates fear completely. When you realise the crisis you are in is not your battle but God's, you act differently, you talk differently, engage differently, walk differently, don't live in panic, and you live with confidence. People who do not understand the source of your confidence will think you are either under the influence of some substance or that you are too proud. Leaders are bold! Leaders act confidently. Leaders go where others will not go. Leaders see what others can't see. David demonstrated these qualities even in the face of a crisis because of the consciousness of the presence of God with him.

[32] 1 Samuel 17:45-46

The battles of life are battles of words. Once you can win the battle of words spiritually, you are bound to win physically. When you know the Word of God and you declare it in the face of that battle, that crisis, you have already won even before the fight. Goliath had been defeated way before the slingshot. David declared that the battle is not his, or even the Israelites. He more or less stepped out of the way for God to do His thing. I always say this, living true to your purpose is giving God expression in your life. When you fulfil your purpose, it is God expressing Himself through you. It's not about you, but God. Remember the words of the scriptures, 'Be still and know that He is God!'[33]

> *"While a crisis is a call to leadership, you must realise that the call is for what God has put on your inside. The call is for the nature, wisdom, and power of God within you."*

While a crisis is a call to leadership, you must realise that the call is for what God has put on your inside. The call is for the nature, wisdom, and power of God within you. It's not a call for your prowess and your natural inclinations. It's a call for God's expression through you. Give that situation over to God. Hand it over to Him. Say, 'Lord, this situation is beyond my control. It's no longer my battle but yours. Come and have your way and do that which You alone can do.' Whenever you pray like this, God is pleased. He is moved to act. God is looking for men and women who know how to lead in crisis, people

---

[33] Psalm 46:10

who know how to be still and know He is God. People who know how to live in the consciousness of His presence.

Did God win the battle for David and the Israelites? Yes, He did! One slingshot from David and the stone hit Goliath right between his eyes and fell flat with his face to the ground. Who is a champion before the Lord of Host? Who is a giant before the King of kings? What is a crisis before the God that made the heavens and the earth? Stop trying to use your natural wisdom, just hand that crisis into God's hands and He will supply you with the wisdom, understanding, and strength to act. He said, 'Call to me, and I will answer you, and show you great and mighty things, which you do not know.'[34] A crisis is your opportunity to witness the great and mighty things God can do through you that you had no idea about. A crisis is your opportunity to allow God to express Himself through you and the abilities He has put within you.

I feel like sharing a lot more examples with you from the Bible. There are so many to inspire you to realise that crisis is a call to leadership. I could talk about the story of Gideon, a mighty man who became a coward because of a crisis, but God's revelation of his true identity and purpose caused him to answer that leadership call and through him, Israel was delivered from oppression. I could talk about the story of Daniel when the king of Babylon had a dream he could not interpret and as a result, the lives of the wise men in the land were in danger including Daniel's. But Daniel answered the leadership call posed by that crisis, called God to action, and God expressed Himself through Daniel's ability to interpret dreams and that changed the story and led

---

[34] Jeremiah 33:3

to God's glorification in the land and the lifting of Daniel. Our Lord Jesus Christ also came to the earth because of the crisis caused by the sins of men. His coming was the easiest, but his death on the cross was the answer to the leadership call to save us from our sins. That was the tough part but instead of His will, He gave in to God's will and allowed God to express Himself through Him by leading the way to Calvary to die for us and won the victory both on earth and in hell.

We have examined some biblical examples, let us look at some historical examples outside the Bible to witness this same principle.

HISTORICAL EXAMPLES

The history of the world is full of the accounts of men and women who answered the call to lead in a crisis. They offered their voice and even though they're long dead and gone, they cannot be forgotten because of their roles in difficult times. Like their biblical counterparts, they were humans like you and me, but they were extraordinary and supernatural in the face of crisis. You could glaringly see it was not about them but God expressing Himself through them for them to achieve the feats we read about in the history books. I am reminded of William Arthur Ward's words, 'Adversity causes some men to break, others to break records.' These men and women broke records because they looked adversity in the face and saw the opportunity to overcome! They saw the opportunity to lead, and lead they did!

NON-BIBLICAL EXAMPLES

Martin Luther King Jr. – The American Civil Rights and Freedom Martyr

When you hear the name, whoever you are, white, black, young, or old, it resounds. It resounds the word freedom. One man. One purpose. One heart. He only lived for 39 years (January 15, 1929 – April 4, 1968) and his life made so much impact than those who lived a hundred. Of course, I did not witness his life but his influence lives long after his death. This is the transgenerational impact fulfilling purpose in crisis brings. You can never be forgotten. The grave cannot bury your works. Your life will be too big for death to terminate. Your influence will be too huge for the grave to swallow.

Born to Michael Luther King Jr (later changed his name to Martin) graduated with a Bachelor of Arts degree in 1948.[35] He later attended Crozer Theological Seminary for three years where his leadership ability saw him elected as president of a predominantly white senior class. He completed his doctorate in 1955 from the same seminary.

That same year, he accepted the leadership of the first great Negro (Black) nonviolent demonstration of contemporary times in the United States. His efforts led to the United States' Supreme Court ruling that the laws requiring segregation of Negros on buses were unconstitutional. In 1957, he was elected president of the Southern Christian Leadership Conference, an organisation formed to provide

---

[35] Got my story from:
https://www.nobelprize.org/prizes/peace/1964/king/biographical/

new leadership for the now burgeoning civil rights movement. His root in the Christian faith was firm, but he also followed the operational frameworks of the renowned Mahatma Gandhi. He gave his life and all for his purpose – to see the United States of America become a racist-free country.

On August 28, 1963, he led the march in Washington for jobs and freedom where he gave the famous 'I have a dream' speech and the words of that speech resonates to date. Scholars say the speech was a defining moment for the civil rights movement and one of the most notable speeches in the history of the world. He was bold, he was articulate and unyielding to any threats. He was firm in his words and purpose on the day. He referred to the emancipation proclamation which declared the freedom of millions of slaves in America and argued that a hundred years after, the 'Negro still is not free.'

Records have it that during Dr. King's speech, at a time, he stopped reading from his prepared text. He spoke straight from his heart on the theme, 'I have a dream.' Scholars believed those words made Dr. King one of the men who shaped modern America. The most recurrent and quoted line was 'I have a dream that my four little children will one day live in a nation where they will not be judged by the colour of their skin, but by the content of their character. I have a dream today!'[36] No doubt, he had a dream because you could see that dream come true all over the world today.

---

[36] Excel HSC Standard English, p. 108, Lloyd Cameron, Barry Spurr – 2009

Purpose in Crisis | **Samuel Ekundayo**

The other day, I watched the movie Selma on Netflix starring David Oyelowo and Tom Wilkinson. I shed a tear more than once and I was so inspired to pursue my purpose and dreams. How could one man be so resilient, passionate, and purposeful such that he moved a whole nation, not by violence but by the integrity of his character and the responsibility and weight of his leadership? One man! In every crisis and seemingly hopeless situation, God is always looking for one man! God is always looking for one voice. Reminds me of that scripture, 'So I sought for a man among them who would make a wall, and stand in the gap before Me on behalf of the land, that I should not destroy it…'[37] Will you answer that leadership call in the crisis our world is in now? Will you be that man God is counting on to rise and fulfil his purpose?

I want to share the story of another 'one-man' that inspired me so much, Nelson Mandela of South Africa.

Nelson Mandela – Anti-apartheid Leader

Your purpose has a way of standing you out. It has a way of calling you out and distinguishing you. As Dr. Martin Luther King Jr, when you hear the name Nelson Mandela, you think of someone who gave his life for the freedom of generations! Some might see the freedom fight of Nelson Mandela as a contention for the future of South Africa, but I assure you it has great implications for the future of our world at large.

---

[37] Ezekiel 22:30 (NKJV)

Born to the family of Mr. Nkosi Mphakanyiswa Gadla Mandela, his father, Nelson, a social rights activist, was the first black president of South Africa, from 1994 to 1999.[38] Before he became president, he did all he could to contribute his quota to the freedom fight of his people that started way before he was born. He completed his Bachelor of Arts degree through the University of South Africa. He obtained his LLB while in prison through the University of South Africa.

For more than 20 years, he led the peaceful, non-violent anti-apartheid campaign against the South African government and its racist policies. In 1956, Nelson and 150 others were arrested and charged for treason for their political advocacy but they were soon set free. When it appeared as though the non-violent campaign was no longer working, history has it that Nelson started to lead some armed offshoot of his political party on the same vision and mission. Following leading a three-day national workers' strike, he was arrested and sentenced to prison. He spent a total of 27 years (from 1962 to 1990) in prison for political offenses, but he did not give up his fight to see his people free. He was also incarcerated on Robben Island for 18 of his 27 years in prison. While in prison, he completed his Bachelor of Law degree through a University of London correspondence program.

On February 11, 1990, Nelson Mandela was freed. Four years later, he became the first Black president of South Africa and fought for a united South Africa. With his influence, in 1996, Mandela signed into law a new constitution that ensured a strong central government based on

---

[38] Source: https://www.nelsonmandela.org/content/page/biography

majority rule that guarantees both the rights of minorities and freedom of expression. What a life!

3

Exercise Your Dominion

YOU WERE MADE FOR DOMINION

Our primary responsibility is to have dominion over the earth's resources. We were made to reign over all that God has created. The very first blessing or gift God gave to man is dominion. He pronounced on us the ability to dominate and manage the resources in it.

This means, crisis or no crisis, you were not made to be ruled by anything on earth. Instead, you were made to rule over everything else. Nothing should control you, you were made to control everything. While a crisis makes most people lose control, panic, and live in uncertainty, when you have this understanding, you will live confidently.

The best time to have this understanding is not during crisis but way before it. If you have been exercising your dominion way before a crisis when it comes, be it global (as in the form of a pandemic) or local (in your own life), it will be too late. You will be well advanced in your ability to manage God's resources and your dominion will see you through the time of crisis.

DOMINION IS NOT OWNERSHIP

The Hebrew word for dominion used in Genesis 1:28 is the word *'radah'* which means to rule. To rule is not the same thing as 'to own'. We are given dominion and authority, but we do not own the resources we have been given to rule over. In other words, dominion is not ownership, it is responsibility. It is a management responsibility.

In God's mandate for dominion, you and I were given the responsibility to manage all of God's resources on earth. Anything you are given to manage, you have to account for. If it's not yours, then you are just a caretaker. I remember the words of the Bible in Genesis 2, in verse 5, it's made clear that God did not send rain on the earth because there were no people to manage/cultivate the soil. So, God delayed rain until He made man.

We all have to give an account of all we have been given to manage. We must not fail in this responsibility because things go very wrong when we fail in our responsibilities to manage God's resources on earth.

YOU LOSE ANYTHING YOU CANNOT EFFECTIVELY MANAGE

Again, dominion means effectively managing God's resources in your life. When you effectively manage the resource God has given you, that's when you are exercising your dominion. The truth is, anything you don't know how to manage, you will lose. This is why many people are not exercising their dominion. They simply do not know how to manage the resources God has put in their disposal.

amuel Ekundayo_

This reminds me of the parable of the talents in the Bible [Matthew 25]. In the parable, a Master (God) gave to some men some resources (talents) to manage for Him while He went away on a journey. He gave to the first one, five talents, another, three talents, and the last one, He gave one talent. The first one used wisely the five talents he was given and got five more talents. The second one traded with his two talents and got two back. The last one decided he was going to hide his and got nothing back in return.

When the Master returned, what He did was amazing. He congratulated the first and the second for their diligence in managing their talents and trading with them. What got me was that He did not sympathise with the one who failed to trade his. He collected the only talent he had and gave it to the man that now had ten talents and made this very important statement: 'To those who use well what they are given, even more will be given, and they will have an abundance. But those who do nothing, even what little they have will be taken away'! [39]

> *"When you effectively manage the resource God has given you, that's when you are exercising your dominion."*

Anything you fail to manage effectively, you will eventually lose. This is a principle. It doesn't matter where on earth you live, it works! If you manage effectively the resources you have been given, you will get more resources. If you manage poorly what you have been given, you will lose potential resources you were supposed to get.

---

[39] Matthew 25:29 NLT

CRISIS IS A REVEALER

A crisis is a revealer of how well you have managed God's resources in your life so far. If you are an effective manager of the resources God has given to you, when a crisis comes, it would be crystal clear because you would have enough resources to thrive and even live in abundance during the crisis. But, if you have been a bad or poor manager, a crisis will plunder you into the pit of lack, penury, and poverty. During a crisis is when that statement the Master (God) made in the last section happens. People who exercise their dominion before a crisis will be blessed with more resources in the crisis.

> *"A crisis is a revealer of how well you have managed God's resources in your life so far."*

This reminds me of the story of Joseph in Egypt. Joseph was still in prison when Pharaoh the king had a dream of an impending crisis.[40] There was going to be seven years of famine in Egypt. But before that, there would be seven years of plenty with lots of wheat with no room to contain harvest. But right after those seven years, there would be seven years of drought and famine. The famine will be so bad that Egyptians will not even remember the initial seven years of plenty. So, if the resources in those seven years of plenty are not well managed, Egyptians will suffer.

The instruction to Pharaoh was to look for a wise and discerning man to put in charge of the resources of the land. Of course, Pharaoh chose Joseph. What a great decision! What Joseph did was remarkable. He

---

[40] Genesis 41

saved the entire Egyptian race by helping them to effectively store up when they had plenty so that by the time famine came, they not only survived, they thrived such that other neighbouring nations came begging for food and they still had more to give.

You see what I mean? Crisis is a revealer of your management-ability. Speaking of management, there are resources that God has given to every man that must be managed carefully – our gifts.

4

Where Is Your Focus?

How do you stay peaceful during a crisis, how do you stay hopeful in a storm? In a time of crisis, many people are full of fear, laden with so much doubt, and uncertainty. But there is a way to stay hopeful, peaceful, and even creative in crisis. The key lies in your focus. During a crisis, it is important to be mindful of your focus. If your focus is on the storm, if you are not careful, the storm will sink you. But if you get your focus right, you will thrive.

The Bible says, 'You will keep him in perfect peace whose mind is fixed on you because he trusts in you.'[41] To be peaceful in a time of crisis, in a time of adversity, is to maintain the right focus. It is to make sure your focus does not shift away from God. If your focus is fixed on God, you will realise you will always be above the storm.

This reminds me of two stories in the Bible. The first was the story of Peter walking on water[42], which is a popular story Bible students know very well. Jesus had asked His disciples to get into the boat after speaking to a crowd of people. He went to pray on the mountain after giving the instruction and told them He would meet them on the other side. While the disciples were on that journey, in the night, a massive

---

[41] Isaiah 26:3
[42] Matthew 14:22-33

storm hit them, right in the middle of the sea, and Jesus was not yet with them. The wind was against them and they were very afraid. It was lonely, dark, and very boisterous. Jesus had to walk on water seeing what was going on from afar. He came close to them and they all thought He was a ghost. They cried out in fear and Jesus had to respond, 'Don't be afraid, I am the one.'

> *"To be peaceful in a time of crisis, in a time of adversity, is to maintain the right focus."*

Peter, quite outspoken, said, 'Jesus, if you are the one, tell me to come to join you on the water.' 'Come', Jesus replied and in no time, Peter started to walk on water like Jesus. One thing we need to bear in mind at this time is that the storm was still going on. This means that at this particular point in history, Peter had completely lost focus of the wind. His focus was on Jesus! This is a powerful principle that is worth studying for days! Peter was not moved by the storm because He had his eyes fixed on Jesus! He was talking to Jesus the whole time and as a result, amid the crisis, he was thriving. He was on top of the crisis because he did not have his mind on the crisis.

I learnt something else from the scripture. Peter's focus determined his level of faith or fear. You see, faith and fear are glaring opposites. Fear and faith cannot co-exist in the same space. They are mutually exclusive. The moment you entertain fear, faith leaves the room. Similarly, the moment you allow faith to take over, fear packs its suitcases, and off it goes. This is why it is important to be conscious in any situation you find yourself whether you are allowing faith to rule you or fear.

'Faith comes by hearing and hearing the word of God.'[43] The very same way faith comes, fear also comes. Faith comes through the things we allow to get into us in forms of what we hear or see. This is why it is important not to live by sight but by faith. Your natural eyes must not dominate your life. You must engage your faith such that what you see physically does not affect what you see or know spiritually about your situation. You may naturally see a crisis, but by faith, you should experience the peace of God that surpasses understanding and let that reign within you. You may naturally be going through a season of lack, loss, failure, but see the future God has for you with the eyes of faith. By faith, you can receive God's Word which completely contradicts what you are going through, and literally, that is what faith is all about. 'Faith, is the substance of things hoped for, the evidence of things unseen.'[44] We cannot see it with our physical eyes, but we believe it exists and as a result, we take the corresponding action.

> *"Do you know that God is always speaking, even in crisis? Are you listening in for His voice or you are listening to other competing voices?"*

Hearing God's Word constantly fuels our faith. The word of Jesus that Peter heard was the fuel for his faith to join Jesus on the water. Do you know that God is always speaking even in crisis? Are you listening in for His voice or you are listening to other competing voices? I can tell you categorically that if you are listening to other voices during a season of crisis, they will fuel your fear and drown your faith. But when you

---

[43] Romans 10:17
[44] Hebrew 11:1

choose to feed yourself with the Word of God and you let your focus be on Him, even in the midst of crisis, like Peter, you will break records and make history. This reminds me of the quote of William Arthur Ward which says, 'Adversity causes some men to break and others to break records.' The secret to breaking records amid adversity is to never give in to the voices that fuel your fear but to listen only to the voice of God that fuels your faith. When your faith is up, you go up, but when your fear is up, you can only go down! When you demonstrate faith, you function in the supernatural – you do that which Jesus is can do!

> *"The secret to breaking records amid adversity is to never give in to the voices that fuel your fear but to listen only to the voice of God that fuels your faith."*

During a storm, we must have the right focus. We are admonished in the scriptures to fix our 'thoughts on what is true, and honourable, and right, and pure, and lovely, and admirable. Think about things that are excellent and worthy of praise.'[45] It is impossible to have your mind on these things and a crisis will sink you. If your focus is on the news, the economy of your country or that of the world, your bank account, the unemployment rate, all that is happening around you, and what people are saying on social media, you will be too afraid and if you are not careful, you will have a panic attack.

Fear will sink you, but faith will make you walk on the very storms that should scare you. When people are afraid, they make the wrong decisions because it is the fear that controls their decision-making

---

[45] Philippians 4:8 (NLT)

process. But when you are full of faith, you are optimistic and as a result, you can make better decisions. The people around you may not understand, but you will be operating from a different reality, a completely different realm. This is why I love the words of Jesus when He said, 'Peace I leave with you; my peace I give you. I do not give to you as the world gives. Do not let your hearts be troubled and do not be afraid.'[46] When we are full of faith, we enjoy a dimension of peace that is not common.

> *"The secret to breaking records amid adversity is to never give in to the voices that fuel your fear but to listen only to the voice of God that fuels your faith."*

This reminds me of one time when Jesus was on the boat with his disciples and a massive storm threatened their lives[47]. They were struggling for survival. Water was already getting into the boat and it was only a matter of time for them to start sinking. But something strange was recorded from that experience. Jesus was asleep on the same boat! Can you believe it? Not only that, but He was also sleeping comfortably on a pillow. I mean, who sleeps during a life-threatening storm? Who sleeps amid a crisis? Are you supposed to even be able to sleep in a crisis like that? The day I came across this scripture, I was shocked! I asked these very same questions too. All of a sudden I heard in my spirit, *Jesus lived in a different reality*! WOW! The only reason you can be peaceful so much that you would even sleep on a pillow is if whatever is happening around you is not getting to you. And the only

---

[46] John 14:27
[47] Mark 4:35-41

way for a storm not to get to you is if your reality to be worlds apart from that storm. Jesus lived in a kingdom where a crisis does not exist. In the kingdom of God, a crisis does not exist.

How do you live in a kingdom like that? You guessed it – BY FAITH! If you are a child of God, your faith qualifies you to live in this kingdom. Your reality will be different from those around you. While others are clamouring for their lives, you will be smiling. While others are terrified, you will be dancing. While others are confused and hopeless, you will be full of confidence that you and your family are safe because God watches over you. This was why Jesus slept so peacefully, unperturbed by the storm, unperturbed by the news, unperturbed by the terror, completely oblivious to the life-threatening situation. What a reality!

Jesus had a different focus from the rest of those on the boat. He was tuned into His spirit at the time. He was probably just enjoying a revelation of Him and His father and did not even have any inclination whatsoever of all that was happening around Him. I can almost hear you say, 'Isn't that insensitive'? You are right. Faith desensitises you to the chaos around you. Faith is a lifter from a crisis. It's not that the things happening in the crisis won't hit you. I believe Jesus' clothes would have been soaked by the water that got into the boat. Probably even, a few debris flying around would have hit him on the face at some point, but this did not stop or affect His peace.

When your faith is rooted in the reality of the kingdom of God, even if you lose your job in a crisis, you will have a different perspective. You will still have joy. You will still have peace.

Purpose in Crisis | Samuel Ekundayo

In the year 1994, one of my siblings died as a result of a strange sickness. She had been sick for days and we had been going back and forth the hospital, but the sickness was not diagnosed. She eventually died. If I recall correctly, the following morning was a Sunday and my parents were and still are pastors. People were expecting us to be mourning. My Dad said, 'No, we're not mourning, we're going to praise God.' That very morning, Dad still preached a message of hope to the congregation. I did not understand what was going on and my nine-year-old mind could not fathom it. What I did not realise, but have since come to understand, was that we lived and are still living in a different reality. My parents' focus was not on what was happening around them, but on what was happening within them.

> *"A crisis is a situation that is beyond our control, but even in such situations, we can control how we respond."*

I believe one of the greatest power God gave to mankind is the ability to control how you respond to things you cannot control. A crisis is a situation that is beyond our control, but even in such situations, we can control how we respond. It is not what happens to us that often matter in life but how we respond. How we respond is a reflection of our perspective. When we have the perspective of faith, we will respond positively, but when we come from a place of fear, we will make the wrong decisions. This is the very same reason why many people take their lives due to the crisis going on in their lives. What they fail to realise is that crisis is just a season and it will soon pass. You cannot afford to make a permanent decision in a temporary situation. Focus on Jesus, not the storm.

My parents taught me a great lesson that day and till date, I have not forgotten. They taught me how to live by conviction, not by happenstance. I learnt that my resolution and conviction must be greater than my situation. Here is one principle: when you establish your convictions way before a crisis arrives, you will never be moved by the crisis. But when you don't have your convictions established, you will always be pressured to make the wrong decisions.

This is the difference between conformers and transformers. Daniel was an example in the Bible. His enemies had forced the king to make a decree against anyone that would pray to God. Daniel's conviction was too strong to conform. He was not a conformer, but a transformer. He continued to pray regardless of the king's decree. His enemies came for his head and put him into the den of lions. You probably know the story – Daniel got into the den and the lions could not eat him. He got out of the den of lions alive! That was a season of crisis in the life of Daniel. He didn't end his life. His conviction got him through. He was resolved and resolute! He would not give in to pressure from anyone, even the king!

I am also reminded of the three Hebrew men; Shadrach, Meshach, and Abednego[48] around the same period. They had a crisis. The king had made a golden image and ordered that everyone in the land and the neighbouring land bow before it at the sound of the trumpet. The three young men were not conformers, so they refused to bow to the king's image or his pressure. The king said he would put anyone that would not bow into a fiery furnace that would kill instantly. Still, these three

---

[48] Daniel 3:16-28

young men did not budge. They were resolute! They even told the king, with all due respect dear king, 'If we are thrown into the blazing furnace, the God we serve is able to deliver us from it, and He will deliver us from Your Majesty's hand. But even if He does not, we want you to know, Your Majesty, that we will not serve your gods or worship the image of gold you have set up.'[49] You can sense the resolution and conviction from the way they spoke to the king, albeit respectfully. They were not ready to succumb to the king's pressure. This got the king very furious. You would think the fury of the king would put fear in the minds of the young men. Not at all! They remained resolute in the face of a crisis up to the point of being thrown into the fire.

> *"If you lose everything, please don't lose your faith amid a fiery storm."*

They did not give up their convictions because of a life-threatening or seemingly hopeless situation. They believed God. Their faith was unshakable. They were resolute! They were ready for anything that would happen. Oh! And did God prove Himself? Faith works! If you lose everything, please don't lose your faith amid a fiery storm. If you lose everything, don't lose your hope. If you lose everything, don't lose your conviction in God. He always shows up even in the toughest of times. During a crisis is a perfect time to ask God to show Himself to you.

Yes, God showed up. He was present in the fire with the three young men. He appeared in the fire. Just as he promised in His words, 'When

---

[49] Daniel 3:17-18 (NIVUK)

you walk through the fire, you will not be burned; the flames will not set you ablaze.'[50] I don't know the kind of crisis you are in right now. I don't know how hot and fiery it is, but one thing I know is that God does not abandon His own in a crisis. You will not be burned, as long as you remain resolute in your faith and your focus is on Jesus, and not the crisis. What the young men did revolutionised their entire generation. The king commanded that no one dares speak against the God of the young men throughout the land. Do you see how your faith and focus can change your story? Don't give up. It is important not to shift focus even if the crisis becomes life-threatening.

Back to the story of Peter. Peter joined Jesus on water, but after a while of enjoying the walk on water, his focus shifted. He changed realms and realities. He exchanged his faith for fear and then he began to sink. Faith in crisis will make you take the next step (that was why Peter could step out of the boat and walked towards Jesus) but fear will halt your steps. Faith unleashes the supernatural and the impossible, but fear will make you only do the possible. When Peter exchanged his faith for fear, he lost the supernatural. He could no longer take the next step. His steps came to a halt, and not only that, he began to sink with the crisis. That is dangerous.

> *"It is important not to shift focus even if the crisis becomes life-threatening."*

Your focus in times of crisis matters a lot. If your focus is on Jesus, all you need is a little faith and you will overcome the crisis. But if your

---

[50] Isaiah 43:2c (NIV)

focus is not on Jesus, even a little fear will sink you. Faith makes it easy to obey God because you trust Him, but fear incapacitates your hearing of God's word in times of crisis.

Peter beckoned Jesus as he was beginning to sink and Jesus delivered him. Even if you have shifted focus before now, I have good news. Jesus is still able to rescue you. It is never too late to call on Jesus. Peter knew this secret even though he had begun to sink. Little faith is better than no faith. What Peter demonstrated there was little faith and that faith saved him. Remember, 'If you have faith as a mustard seed, you will say to this mountain, 'Move from here to there,' and it will move; and nothing will be impossible for you.' [51] Nothing will be impossible for you if you have faith, no matter how small.

I wrote this chapter to remind you or let you know that your focus is very important in the face of crisis. Don't look at the storm, don't see the difficulty, instead look to Jesus. Keep your gaze on Him. Don't shift your stand. Remain resolute to your conviction and faith no matter how tough things might look, even if the crisis is life-threatening. God can save and deliver you as we saw in those examples. A crisis is a great time for God to prove Himself in our lives.

---

[51] Matthew 17:20

5

Opportunity In Adversity

I said earlier that crisis introduces us to opportunities. I know this because I have experienced it. When you learn to look for opportunities in crisis, you will find them and they are capable of transforming your life. When you see a raw gold in the rough, unless you are an expert whose eyes have been trained to spot one, you will never be able to identify it. Experts say that it is possible to see a fake gold and think it is real gold. For instance, real gold can be soft, but one thing is that it does not fall apart when you touch it unless it's a fake or fool's gold. There are many characteristics that experts have to be on the lookout for when panning for true raw gold such as weight, colour, strength, shapes and sizes, brightness. Just as your eyes have to be trained to spot true gold in the rough, your eyes within have to be trained to spot the golden opportunities in crisis.

To help train your eyes, I want to share four of them with you in this book.

OPPORTUNITY FOR CHANGE

A crisis is also an opportunity for change. Sometimes, until change happens, we do not realise what we need to change. No, change is not always palatable. Change is not always very easy. We are often afraid of and skeptical about change. In the words of John Maxwell, 'Everybody loves change, but nobody wants to change.' As long as the change does not affect you, you are happy. But the moment the change is going to affect you, you are not happy. You resist change with a massive effort. The truth is that change benefits us. For us to benefit from change is to realise that we have to expect it.

How do you expect to change? It is to understand that change is constant. The job you are doing right now, you're not going to do it forever. The house you're living in right now, you're not going to live in it forever. Change is the only constant thing. The Bible admonishes us that to everything in life, there is a season and a time to every purpose. That means nothing in life lasts very long. There is always change.

Guess what? Change is an opportunity. If you learn to see change as an opportunity as shared in other sections of this chapter (an opportunity to grow, and leave your comfort zone), you will realise that there are many things inside of every change. When seasons come and seasons go, we tend to get into new clothes. We tend to have new experiences. These are all opportunities for us, but if the changes do not happen, then we don't take advantage of these new experiences and all these exciting things that could happen.

Listen to me, you cannot stop change. It is impossible. It is very constant. Change must happen. But how do you deal with it when it happens? How do you look for the opportunities in change? It is to understand change. It is to accept change. Most importantly, accommodate it. Then, adapt to it. Many people don't want to adapt to change. They don't want to accommodate it. They don't want to embrace it. They don't want to accept it, so what they do is fight it. No matter how much you fight change, it will only result to your detriment.

When you learn to embrace change, when you learn to accommodate change, when you learn to understand it and adapt to it, then you will come on top of it. Then, you will overcome it. Nobody knows you for what you have not overcome. When you overcome, that is when you get known. The history book is full of men and women who have overcome adversity, who have overcome change at one time or the other. No matter how insecure you may feel in a time of change, you must realise that change was not meant to destroy you. Change is your opportunity. The key to life is to outlast any change. The key to life is to outlast any season of change. Nothing leads to self-destruction than not wanting to change.

> *"When you learn to embrace change, when you learn to accommodate change, when you learn to understand it and adapt to it, then you will come on top of it."*

The only person that does not change is God. Guess what? God is the God of change. He introduces change all the time. Check out the history of the world. God is a God of change, even though He does not change. So, to fight change is actually to be working against yourself. You must learn to accommodate it, accept it, embrace it, and adapt. That will do you a lot of good.

OPPORTUNITY FOR GROWTH

Crises present us with the opportunity to grow. We don't grow in comfortable times. We don't grow in nice times. We don't grow when things are rosy. No! We grow when things are tough. Have you not heard that 'Tough times never last, but tough people do'? Absolutely! That is a recipe for growth during tough times. A recipe for growth in times of adversity. You must realise that there is something on your inside that is calling out for growth in a time of difficulty. I love the words of William Shakespeare when he said, 'Sweet are the uses of adversity".

> *"You must realise that there is something on your inside that is calling out for growth in a time of difficulty."*

There are opportunities in adversity. Those opportunities are for your growth and growth is the only guarantee that tomorrow will be better. Growth is the only assurance of a colourful future. When we overcome difficult times, we are no longer where we were. We are no longer at the same level. All of a sudden, we are more mature. All of a sudden, we have grown. All of a sudden, we have developed.

You too must take advantage. You must harness that opportunity. You must make a commitment that you are going to grow, despite the crisis. I have come to realise that the things that happen to us happen so that we can grow through them. The things you're going through right now, you must grow through. Don't just go through it, but grow through it. In the words of John Maxwell, 'You don't go into an opportunity, you grow into an opportunity.'

A crisis is your opportunity to identify areas in your life where you must grow. I always advise that people grow in at least two areas: an area of skill and an area of attitude. Look at some of the skills you have right now, and begin to look at where you could be. Begin to identify the skills that you need to be where you could be. What attitude do you need to develop to be where you need to be? When you look at these two areas of your life, begin to use the crisis as the opportunity to begin to grow into those areas, to grow those skills or that attitude that you need for your next level or where you are going to. In case you are going through tough times right now, I don't want you to just be buried, thinking that life is bad, gloomy, and tough. No! I want you to begin to train your eyes for the growth opportunities, even within that crisis.

OPPORTUNITY TO LEAVE OUR COMFORT ZONES

Crises provide an opportunity to leave our comfort zones. Until crises happen, until we get into some form of adversity or some form of 'un-comfortability', we do not realise that we are in our comfort zone. Many of us have been stuck, for a long time, in our comfort zones. We do the jobs that appear to be too easy. We do things that appear to fit within the boundaries of what we seemingly enjoy. There is no opportunity to grow, but we are just happy where we are. That is a comfort zone. Many of us have been stuck in that place for a very long time. What a crisis does is to shake us up. It is to help us realise that there is much more to us, that we could be more, live more, be more, and become more. When a crisis happens at times like that, we can come out of those comfort zones and begin to use those uncomfortable situations to reach out for the things that are ahead of us, or to reach out for the greatness that is within us.

"Crises provide an opportunity to leave our comfort zones."

I remember at a particular point in time, I was doing an IT support job in New Zealand where I live. I was enjoying the money, but what I did not realise was that I was being underpaid until a crisis showed up. My boss suddenly did not like me anymore. He started micromanaging me. The usual 'Staff of the Month' award that I would always get just seemingly became impossible. It appeared that I was no longer being celebrated, I was only being tolerated in the office. But that crisis made me realise my value. It made me realise that I was stuck in my comfort zone. It made me realise that I needed to do something to grow and get out of that place, so I began to do something. The more I looked out and began to look at opportunities around me, the more I started to realise that I was being underpaid and undervalued. I started to apply for other positions. As I got to the interviews, I found out some of the things that I could be doing that I was not doing where I was. I realised some of the growth levels I could ascend to that I was not getting to where I was. I was astounded! I began to thank God for the crisis. Guess what? After a few interviews, I realised that I was supposed to be paid at least double what I was earning. My goodness! I remember not getting a particular job because they thought I was overpaid for a salary that was double what I was earning in my comfort zone. It took the crisis, the enmity from my boss, the tough situation, and the adversity, for me to be able to lunge out.

No wonder William Arthur Ward said, 'Adversity causes some men to break, others, to break records.' It was an opportunity for me to break records. As soon as I broke out of that place, I started to realise the many opportunities to leave my comfort zone. Guess what? I was able to leave my comfort zone to a much better job, begin a new career as a Business Analyst, and earn more than I was earning – double what I was earning.

> *"I often believe that crises, or the times of adversity and problems, are what introduce us to the leadership ability on our inside; either to lead ourselves or to lead other people."*

You too may be stuck where you are right now. Everything may be sweet and rosy, but when a crisis hits, I want you to have a different perspective. Maybe a crisis has hit. Maybe you are in a crisis right now. There is a perspective I want you to pitch into. That is, there is something beyond your comfort zone. There is growth, development, an opportunity for you to be able to realise your value. There is an opportunity to realise the value that you carry and to realise that you are worth much more. To realise that you can reach out for something bigger and better.

OPPORTUNITY TO LEAD

A crisis also presents an opportunity to lead. What is leadership? In the words of John C. Maxwell, 'Leadership is influence. Nothing more, nothing less.' What is influence? Influence is the capacity to affect the character, development, or behaviour of someone. That means in crisis, you have the opportunity to influence other people, or perhaps influence yourself. When you influence yourself, it is personal leadership. I often believe that crises, or the times of adversity and problems, are what introduce us to the leadership ability on our inside; either to lead ourselves or to lead other people.

I'm reminded of the story of David. At a particular point in time, he had taken his whole army to war. While they were fighting their war, another war was happening in their house that they did not know about. The enemy had come to cart away their wives, and their children. By the time they returned home and were supposed to be celebrating their victory, they realised another defeat had happened. Their wives and children had been carted away. I remember, according to the words of the Scripture, David was so discouraged and down cast in his soul. He was fighting a war that God had encouraged him to fight, so when that happened he was so down cast and the men that were with him wanted to stone him. What they did not realise was that David was also a partaker of the adversity and crisis. His wives and children had been carted away too, but they wanted to stone him. They were blaming him for what had happened. But something happened, which the Bible recorded, that we have to study for days. The Bible says that 'David encouraged himself in the Lord his God.' Wow! What other way can you describe personal leadership other than that? To be able to encourage yourself amid crisis. To be able to find encouragement from within. Powerful! That's personal leadership.

Because David was able to find encouragement from within, guess what? He was able to encourage those without. Because he was able to encourage himself, he encouraged the men who initially wanted to stone him, and they were able to unite themselves to go to war again. They got their wives and their children back.

I don't know what you are going through while reading this book. I don't know what you are going through that is very tough for you. But one thing that I know that is very clear is that you can encourage yourself. You have the capacity. You have the intestinal fortitude to be able to influence yourself in personal leadership so that you can influence others. So that you can be the beacon of hope, light, and faith even to other people, no matter what they are going through. I believe that you can spot that opportunity to lead even in the times of crisis. I believe in you.

6

How To Discover Your Purpose?

One of life's most important questions to ask yourself is: WHY AM I HERE? The late Dr. Myles Munroe said, 'In order to be successful, a man must ask himself five questions and WHY AM I HERE? is one of those life's defining questions.' This is a life-defining question because everything in life begins and ends with purpose. Your purpose is the only thing that gives meaning to life and makes you relevant in your generation and the ones after you.

I am convinced that one of the most important journeys a man can ever embark on is the journey of purpose discovery. John Maxwell said, 'There are two objectives of man – to find himself and to lose himself.' To find yourself is to discover why you were created and born. To lose yourself is to commit that purpose into something bigger than you. When you are living for something bigger than you, you are not afraid of death. The truth is, what we are living for and what we are dying for is essentially the same thing. In the words of Dr. Martin Luther King Jr., 'If a man hasn't found something he will die for, he isn't fit to live.' To be fit to live is to find what to die for. That's your purpose.

It is important to realise that you can find your purpose and many times, your purpose comes looking for you, calling out your name. Moses was in a rush to enter into his purpose, but when God was ready,

He called out to Moses in a burning bush experience. In the next few pages, I will be sharing with you my PURPOSE DISCOVERY FRAMEWORK™.

PURPOSE DISCOVERY FRAMEWORK™

Following several years of study, I emerged with this framework that proposes that there are six different places to look to get cues to our purposes. In my life's experience and the discovery of my purpose, I have seen these six directions feature, so what I will be sharing is real and if you look too, I am sure you will either find your purpose or realise it's been calling out to you all the while. Now, a small disclaimer here: I am not claiming this framework is exhaustive in helping you discover your purpose, but it will help point you in the right direction, challenge existing beliefs, and provide you with cues to find your purpose.

As a person of faith, I believe only God can directly reveal our purposes to us. I mean that purpose is the reason for the creation of a thing, which means the only person that knows the true purpose of anything is the creator of that thing. So, this framework is by no means competing with God's sovereignty in light of seeking Him for your purpose, but I believe God leaves clues and cues to our purpose throughout our lives and this framework will create an epiphany, a lightbulb moment, that will stir up a desire to get clarity in the place of prayer. Now, let's discuss the six directions to look for cues to your purpose:

> *"It is important to realise that you can find your purpose and many times, your purpose comes looking for you, calling out your name."*

A. Look Up

The first and the surest place to look to discover your purpose is UP! By looking up, I mean going directly to your Creator, the Creator of all things – GOD!

In the year 2016, I had an encounter that completely changed my life. I was beginning to ask a very pertinent question, following three years of holding a Ph.D., 'Is this all there is to life?' Having a Ph.D. at the time was a long term dream and now that it had come true, I found myself asking, 'Is this all there is to life?' At that very time as well, I heard a sermon that changed my life; the preacher said, 'All of you in this room who are multitalented, you need to realise that you will account for all the gifts and talents that God has given you because to whom much is given, much is also expected.' It was as if he was talking directly to me. That sermon got me scared. I ran to God and started seeking His face asking, 'Lord, all these gifts and abilities you have given me are for what purpose?' After many days of seeking God's face, praying, fasting, and meditating on the Word of God, I heard a word in my spirit one afternoon, 'Help people discover their purpose.' I took those words very seriously and ran with it. I realised God created me so I could help others discover their purposes. I became very clear about my assignment in life. I was so certain that I quit most things I was involved in at the time to help me focus on my life's calling. That was the experience that led to the discovery of my purpose.

You too can have a similar experience. If you are a person of faith, I challenge you to seek the face of God in prayer. Even if you are in crisis, you can ask God to show you His purpose for your life. If you are committed to the process and are serious about hearing God, He will speak to you in the way only He can! There are several accounts in the Bible where God spoke to people directly about their purpose.

Saul, who later became Paul, was on his way to Damascus on an errand that was opposite what he was created to do, and he encountered God in the process. He was then redirected after several days of spending time in God's presence to his real purpose. Moses too had a burning bush experience where God spoke to him about his life's purpose and that was the defining moment in Moses' life – that single experience!

> *"The first and the surest place to look to discover your purpose is UP! By looking up, I mean going directly to your Creator, the Creator of all things – GOD. "*

I invite you to look up today as you're reading this book. Take it upon yourself to seek the face of God asking Him to show you why He created you and you will be amazed at what this experience will do to you and how it will completely change your life forever. I promise you, it's a life-changing experience. If you are not a person of faith, there are other ways you can look to find cues to your purpose, but I want to invite you to consider this moment a defining moment by asking God to reveal to you. But first, you have to accept Him into your life as your Lord and Saviour and then He will start talking to you as His own. It's a life-changing experience when God speaks to you, trust me.

You can also look within you for a cue to your purpose. I will share more on this with you in the next section.

B. Look Within

There are some inherent gifts, talents, and passions that each of us are blessed with. They came with you. You were born with them. I am not referring to the skills you learnt in school. I am talking about the things you do naturally that if you are not paid for, you would so gladly and passionately do for FREE. Those gifts come with a natural zeal, fire, excitement, and intensity that you feel when you are actively using them.

From a very young age, I realised my gift of speaking and writing. In fact, around the age of 17, I finished a manuscript for a book that I wanted to publish. The manuscript got lost in the hands of a family friend I asked to help review it. Moreover, around those times I was part of the literature and debating society in my high school. I would go with my colleagues for public speaking competitions and we would win.

A particular teacher of mine, Mrs. Oni by name, recognised this gift in me. At the time, she saw that I had the inherent gift of speaking, but my accent was not very polished. So, she decided she was going to help me polish it. I remember one day she came into our classroom, called me and a few other students to the staff room. She handed us a paper with topics to debate on impromptu. She had not given us time to prepare and she asked us to start speaking. When it was my turn, and I opened my mouth, the entire staff room started laughing, except Mrs. Oni. She did not find it funny, instead, she challenged my accent and showed me how I could speak better. She took it upon herself to help me refine the gift by polishing my accent as we would be attending various competitions with students from more refined backgrounds with polished accents. She wanted me to be able to measure up. All my life, I will always be grateful to Mrs. Oni for discovering that gift in me when I could not see it in myself. We attended various competitions under the leadership of Mrs. Oni and came back with certificates and prizes.

Since then, I knew I had the inherent gift within me to speak. The confidence to speak comes naturally. You can wake me up from sleep and ask me to speak on one of my favourite topics and without preparing, I will go on for days making sense. It's a natural ability. I don't have to struggle, I don't have to hustle. I am just a born communicator. In fact, in Singapore, a foreign land my family moved to in 2006, I participated in an International Toastmasters Competition. We went through a series of auditions and group stages before the grand finale. As a foreigner, I never believed I stood a chance, but friends encouraged me to keep going. I scaled through all the auditions and group stages and was one of the finalists.

The D-Day came and you needed to see the other awesome finalists. A few of them spoke before me and truthfully, I had counted myself out because those speakers were awesome and without speaking, I would have given them the cup because they were amazing. But, by the time I got up to speak, the atmosphere changed. The room went silent. You could hear a pin drop. Everyone listened with rapt attention. No one looked left or right, their gaze was on me the whole time. I remember speaking on the topic:

WHO ARE YOU AND WHERE ARE YOU GOING?

By the time I was done, there was grand applause like they gave to everyone but I didn't know mine was different. The other finalists spoke and they were awesome too. In the end, the moderator of the final came in to announce the winners. She started from the second runner up, my name was not mentioned. She mentioned the first runner up and still, my name was not mentioned. I said to myself, 'You didn't win.' I had begun consoling myself. To my utmost shock and amazement, she announced, 'And the winner is Samuel Ekundayo with the topic, Who Are You And Where Are You Going?' I nearly passed out! It was a major competition and I didn't see it coming even though I prepared so much for it. That experience confirmed speaking for me is a gift I was born with and I know I just have to share it with the world.

> *"These things you can naturally do are pointers to your purpose."*

Similarly, for my writing, I once had a blog that had about 10,000 visitors monthly from all over the world. And at a point, if I remember correctly, around 2010 or so, I was awarded the Most Inspiring Blog in Nigeria. I want to believe such awards can only be possible if you're gifted or have a passion for writing and inspiring people with your writing. I shared my story because I want you to take an introspective look into your life as well, what are those things that come to you so naturally? What are those things you do like you have been supremely and divinely qualified to? What is that thing that if you are woken up from sleep, you would still do so graciously and excellently even if you did not prepare? That thing is your gift or talent. It is important to realise this gift is a cue to your purpose.

This is because a function was built into creation for it to serve its purpose. This means these things you can naturally do are pointers to your purpose. The more you do them, the more you find the world is drawn to you, you grow in influence, and you become sought after. I agree, the gift will have to be refined for it to become valuable, but even without any refinement, you could already see, this is a natural gift, talent, or passion because it flows out of you naturally.

There is an area of life that God has given you dominion in. You are like a king in that sphere! The word 'Dominion' comes from the word 'Domain'. All of us are kings in our domain. For you to become a person of influence and fulfil your purpose, you have to find that domain and exercise dominion there, otherwise you will live an ordinary life and die unknown. Yours could be music, poetry, cooking, design, coding, dancing, counselling, painting, entrepreneurship, public speaking, preaching, arts, whatever it is, you have to find it.

Have you found those natural gifts that flow naturally out of you yet? If you haven't, I invite you to take the next few days to look within and pay attention to your findings.

Theory of Multiple Intelligences

In 1983, Dr. Howard Gardner, a professor of education at Harvard University in his book, *Frames of Mind: The Theory of Multiple Intelligences*, posited that the traditional notion of intelligence that is based on IQ testing is too limited to define the limitless nature of the human potential. In his work, he proposed nine different bits of intelligence that I believe point to the unexhaustive range of human potential in both children and adults. These multiple intelligence (nine of them) give clarity to our inherent gifts – things that come to us so naturally to reflect what we're 'graced' to do. In the various places I have been privileged to speak and deliver my purpose discovery and clarity workshops and training, I have shared them and they have liberated lives.

I am sharing them in this chapter because many people have been defeated as a result of the grades they got from our educational systems. Listen, those grades do not define who you are and do not determine whether you are intelligent or not. As you will soon find out, the truth is, our education system often only measure logical-mathematical and linguistic intelligence as if they are the only forms of intelligence, but this is not true. The human potential is not limited to these two types of intelligence. Thanks to the work of Howard Gardner, we can see that there is more to the human potential beyond the IQ tests and the various assessments used in our educational systems. So, if you have failed Mathematics and English Language during your days as a student or maybe you are failing them right now, I have brought you good news. Your human potential is not limited to those subjects alone.

Let us examine those bits of intelligence so that you can see that within you lie incredible potentials that the world has not developed any system adequate to measure. They include:

1. **Linguistic Intelligence**: This refers to people who are word and language smart. They just always seem to have the right words

to express what they mean. They are very eloquent and oratory by nature. People with this type of intelligence are typically good at reading, writing, telling stories, and memorising words. When you look at people like President Barrack Obama, Tony Robbins, Dr. Martin Luther King Jr., you are easily able to see this type of intelligence shine through.

2. **Logical-Mathematical Intelligence:** This refers to people who are numbers or reasoning smart. These are critical thinkers and they are capable of making logical abstractions. They just know their way around quantifying things and enjoy making hypotheses and proving them. Names like Albert Einstein comes to mind here. He discovered $E=mc^2$. He logically proved that Energy and Mass are the same. I mean, this is a gift!

3. **Spatial Intelligence:** This refers to people who are picture smart. They can think and visualise the world in three-dimensions. They can solve spatial problems of navigation by looking at objects from various angles, faces, and scenes to notice fine details that are not visible to the common man. These are Engineers, Sculptors, Pilots, Architects, Artists, and so on. The names Leonardo da Vinci and Pablo Picasso come to mind here.

4. **Bodily-Kinesthetics Intelligence**: This refers to people who are 'body smart'. They have the gift to easily coordinate their mind with their body. They can control their bodily motions and responses to perform physical activities such as acting, sports, dance, and so on. I love football and whenever I watch Cristiano Ronaldo and Lionel Messi, I think of their masterful

prowess of handling the ball and it could only be that they are body-smart.

5. **Musical Intelligence**: This refers to people who are music smart. They can discern sounds, pitch, tone, frequencies, rhythm, and timbre. Something common to these groups of people is that they are sensitive listeners. When you think of Beethoven and Mozart, you understand what I am talking about.

6. **Interpersonal Intelligence**: This refers to people who are 'people smart'. They have the inherent gift and ability to connect with and interact effectively with others. Be it verbal or non-verbal communication, they are sensitive to others' moods and as a result, they can easily impart, entertain, and connect with people, especially an audience. When you meet naturally gifted Teachers, Actors, Politicians, you would easily see the gift or intelligence shine through.

7. **Intrapersonal Intelligence**: This refers to people who are 'self-smart'. It's an incredible inherent ability to understand one's thoughts, feelings, and channel such knowledge to lead one's life. These people are often naturally self-motivated. Psychologists, Coaches, Spiritual leaders, Philosophers tend to fall into this category.

8. **Naturalist Intelligence:** This refers to people who are 'nature smart'. These people have a natural love for all or most things nature – plants, animals, clouds, rock configurations, oceans, etc. They possess the instinct to distinctly tell the differences

between various plant types and rock configurations. Chefs and Botanists are the ones that have this type of intelligence.

9. **Existential Intelligence:** These are people we refer to as 'life smart'. Naturally, these people can tackle life's tough and deep questions about human existence including the meaning of life, why humans exist, and so on. Most spiritual leaders have this type of intelligence. I believe I am one of them.

When you consider these nine bits of intelligence, which do you think you have so naturally? I am sure you can relate to at least one.

Temperaments

Beyond inherent gifts, your temperaments could also be cues to your purpose. In His book, *Why You Act The Way You Do*, Tim Lahaye argues that our actions and behaviours are determined by a complete network of traits we inherit from our parents, which he referred to as temperaments. He argued that there are four dominant temperaments. They are:

1. **Sanguine:** These people are spontaneous, high-spirited, and attractively lively. They are naturally optimistic people and tend to see the positives in things. Once a sanguine enters a dull environment, they lift the atmosphere by adding joy and life. They are the life of the party and are not afraid to be the centre of attention anywhere they find themselves.

2. **Melancholy:** They are naturally thoughtful, loyal, and persistent individuals. Quite attentive to detail and tend to have high standards that see them achieving a lot in their fields of

discipline. They can be very organised and conscientious by nature and for them, if something is worth doing, it's worth doing very well.

3. **Choleric:** They are naturally confident, compelling, and adventurous. Goal setters and risk-takers by nature, as a result, they have a plan for almost everything. They are naturally motivated to take on tasks that are labelled impossible or difficult, as a result, they may appear to be insensitive to people's feelings as long as goals are being achieved.

4. **Phlegmatic:** They are people who just go with the flow. They always need to be persuaded or perhaps even coaxed to focus on their own needs. They are pretty relaxed and laid back, often requiring motivation and inspiration from others to make decisions and achieving goals.

Interestingly, some of us have a combination of these temperaments. I am sanguine-choleric by nature. If you have met me before, you would know I am a naturally spontaneous and highly spirited individual. I am usually the life of the party, the centre of attention anywhere I am. Those are the sanguine parts of me. And then the choleric in me is naturally wanting to lead the way and can be quite confident, no matter where I am or the people I am with. These temperaments are a gift to me by God, though inherited from my parents. They help me fulfil my purpose quite effectively. This is why I can be a coach, speaker, and mentor to many people.

To re-emphasise, our temperaments are gifts to us. No matter your combination of temperaments, you did not decide on your temperaments when you were being created or when you were conceived in the womb of your mother. God carefully chose these traits from your parents and you inherited them. Whether you like it or not, that's your make-up; that's how you have been formed. God knew the right (combination of) temperaments to help you fulfil His purpose for your life. And when you look at your temperaments, you could get some insight into your purpose. This is why I am discussing this under 'Look Within'. Like I said earlier, my combination of sanguine and choleric temperaments are a blessing from God.

> *"God knew the right (combination of) temperaments to help you fulfil His purpose for your life."*

For these gifts, intelligence, and temperaments within us, we have to accept them and take responsibility for us to effectively fulfil our purposes. Some of us are not accepting the gifts, temperaments, and intelligence we have been given by God and this is why many of us are not living the purpose of God for our lives. You have to come to terms with them and accept them so you can begin to leverage them for your success and prosperity.

GOD'S DIMENSION IN YOU

Man is God's most powerful creation because he is also a creator. For instance, God created trees, but He didn't create chairs and tables. He created the cotton tree but didn't make a shirt. He created apples and oranges, but not juice. God created carbon and hydrogen, but he didn't create plastics. He made clay, but he didn't make ceramics. He created only one man and one woman and today we have billions of them in the world - in the different shapes, sizes, and colours.

This means God has given you the capacity to create whatever you want with what He has given you. In other words, if you are in debt today, you can get yourself out. If you are poor today, you can become rich. If you are studying and failing today, that can soon change. You have the power to create the future you want by what God has put on your inside. There is an inherent power within you that is capable of creating seen things from the unseen.

> *"You have the power to create the future you want by what God has put on your inside."*

I love the words of the Bible that say, 'But this precious treasure—this light and power that now shine within us—is held in a perishable container, that is, in our weak bodies. Everyone can see that the glorious power within must be from God and is not our own.' [52] There is something you carry that does not belong to you. There is something you carry that is bigger than you. There is an inherent power on your inside. It is right within you as you read this. It's the power of God. That power is the source of your significance, influence, wealth, prosperity, affluence, and greatness. I call that power

THE DIMENSION OF GOD WITHIN YOU.

There is a dimension of God in every man. In other words, there is a part of God that you carry, His nature within you that gives your life

---

[52] 2 Corinthians 4:7 (TLB)

significance and reinforces your dominion in the world. Allow me to encapsulate this for you visually. See, God is so big and so mighty that He could not put His entire self into one man. And that's not possible because that man will become God (take note of the capital G). So, what God did was divide portions (what I call dimensions) of Himself into every man so that every man has a dimension of God. That way, we all carry a dimension of His nature, power, ability, and creativity. This is the source of our dominion.

"There is something you can do at the level of God."

How do I know this?

The Bible says, 'And the LORD God formed man of the dust of the ground, **and breathed into his nostrils the breath of life; and man became a living soul**.' [53] The last part of that scripture is very powerful. God's impartation of the dimension of Himself into man came about by His breath. By breathing into man, he put a portion of Himself in him. The word 'breath' is transliterated *nasham* in Hebrew meaning divine inspiration, intellect, or spirit. That is powerful. You have the inspiration of God within you. You have His intellect. You have His spirit. I would not want to delve into deep theology in this book as I only want to let you know that you carry a dimension of God on your inside, otherwise, I would have shown you some deep insight about that scripture.

There is a realisation I want this part of the book to give you and it is that there is something each man does at a supernatural level – what I

[53] Genesis 2:7 KJV

often call 'At God level.' Let me personalise it for you. There is something you can do at the level of God. It's not many things! At least one very thing! That power exists in every man and that is why each man is capable of doing something amazing, unique, and unbelievable in at least an area of life. When you find that area of life or domain, you have found the dimension of God on your inside.

Hear this;

There is a dimension of God that is musical. This is why when you hear some people sing, you would be in awe and wonder. Every time I stumble on any documentary of the late Michael Jackson, I am always amazed at how much of the musical dimension of God was in him. At a point, in one of his concerts, people were dying to touch him.

There is a dimension of God that is visionary: The Bible says, He 'creates new things out of nothing' [54] When you look at the story of creation, you would see this trait of God. When you see the artists of our world and watch them bring something beautiful out of nothing, you would easily see this supernatural side of God. When you see how Architects would look at a piece of land and just begin to design an edifice, you can tell it is the dimension of God in them at work.

There is a dimension of God that is full of fashion: When Adam and Eve sinned and they were ashamed because they were afraid and naked, remember who made the first clothes from leaves? Yes! God made the very first cloth from leaves. He is the very author of fashion! You could have this trait in you. It is the nature of God. When you see

---

[54] Romans 4:17

fashion icons creating some colourful and elegant attires, you can tell where they got it from.

There is a dimension of God that is colourful: When you look at the rainbow, you would understand what I am talking about. Not only that, the colours of the sky, the galaxies, the leaves, the sun, the flowers. Such beauty can only come from an awesome God. God is colourful and beautiful by nature.

There is a dimension of God that is scientific: God has already made water before men discovered anything called Hydrogen and Oxygen. He had made salt before men realised salt is a compound composition of Sodium and Chlorine. It is nature. Scientists like Albert Einstein and Thomas Edison and Chemists like Adam Lambert that we celebrate their lives got that nature from God!

There is a dimension of God that is oratory: Every time I look at President Obama or watch Dr. Martin Luther King's videos, I see the supernatural dimension of God's oratory. It's like a force! I see this dimension in my life as well. Many of my talks, by the time I am done, I watch them over again and I am like 'Who is that?' The things I said and the gestures I made, the humour, the eye-contact with people, or the abstractions made from my notes that I never planned, it could only be that dimension of God on my inside.

There is a dimension of God that is meteorological: The Bible speaks of the sons of Issachar who understood times and seasons, and as a result, they knew what to do per time. God gave them the nature of His.

These dimensions of God are in us, around us, in the people we know, in the people we celebrate, some of them long dead and gone, yet that dimension still lives on in their craft, pieces of history that cannot be erased. I believe a major sign of this dimension in the life of anyone is when you do that thing that corresponds with the nature of God in your life and people are in awe. For instance, if you are a fashion designer, and by the time you are done designing an attire and people go WOW! Or if you are a chef and you made a delicious meal second to none, that even when you share the recipe with others, they just can't seem to reproduce your meal the way you have done it.

This dimension of God is the stamp on our uniqueness in the world. My friend, Pastor Oluwaseun Oyeniran, in his book – Live, Love, Learn, Grow – term this 'Divine Original' He advised that if we all tap into the power of solitude, we will access the 'great untapped creative energy/creativity that is yet to be revealed to the world. [55] The dimension of God on your inside is the source of your originality. It helps you to tap into the power of doing something that only you can do the way you do it. Let me explain. Even if there are one million graphic designers in the world, if you are a divine original and that dimension of God is on your inside, your style, your craft will be so unique that no one can do it the way you do, even if you train them and gave away all your secrets. If you are a chef, no one will be able to make the meals you make the way you make it.

---

[55] Live, Love, Learn, Grow (1st Edition) | pg 116 | by Oluwasegun and Channon Oyeniran

When you understand this truth I am sharing with you, you will never have to compete with anyone for anything anymore in life. You will realise that no one carries what you carry. This realisation helps me to understand that, no one can preach the message of purpose, the way I preach it. There are millions of people who talk about purpose every single day but every time I mount a platform offline or online to speak on the topic of purpose, I am not the one doing it, it's the dimension of God on my inside at work. That is why I always say you can compete with the ability of a man but you can never compete with the dimension (or grace) of God on their inside.

I do pray that this chapter of this book will help you come to this life-changing realisation too.

C. Look Down

Another place to look for cues to your purpose is the seemingly negative experiences you have had or currently having in your life. Yes, you read right – the negative experiences in your life can point to your purpose. The same way God uses positive things to help us discern our purposes, He also uses negative things.

I remember when I repeated a class in my high school days, I was so dejected and down. Every day for the next few months was all dark and gloomy. I failed a major exam and the consequence was to repeat the class the following year. It was like my whole world came crashing down. I mean, sitting with my juniors the following year was too much to deal with for me. I could not bear to see that happening. I was distraught but that experience changed my life forever.

Purpose in Crisis | Samuel Ekundayo

It was the one single experience that sort of gave me clarity that I have not been taking my life seriously and that I had been living without purpose and vision. As I prepared for the next year, I remember my parents enrolling me for various extramural classes to help get right the subjects I did not do very well in the failed exam.

As I attended those classes, not only was I starting to understand the things I did not get right or understand, I started to rethink my life, develop a vision for my life, and live determined to succeed. Little did I know that God used that experience for me to learn how to deal with failure and most importantly, help others deal with failure.

Now, as a coach, mentor, speaker, and preacher, one of my favourite things to do is help people see failure differently and deal with it effectively. I feel like I understand perfectly what anyone that has failed has gone or is going through. At the time, I had no idea that it was a cue to my purpose. God used the experience not only to stir me in the right direction but also to prepare me for the destiny he had ahead of me.

So, your 'down' experiences are worth re-examining for the cues to your purpose. If you examine them carefully, you are likely to get a pointer to how God wants to use you to set others in similar situations free now and in the future. All you need to do is step into that zone. I hear stories of people like Tony Robbins who used to be very poor and had no money, but those down experiences are now the inspiration and motivation for others to break free from poverty.

If you have been abused in the past or you are currently going through some form of abuse, could it be that there is a future ahead of you where you will be a mentor, coach, or inspiration to many who are equally being abused? I believe the best mentors are those who have been where you are now and can take you out and bring you to where they are now. Your negative experiences have a major stake in where God is taking you. I do not doubt that.

> *"Your purpose is the source of your value and as a result, the negative experiences in your life do not cancel or reduce your value."*

Your purpose is the source of your value and as a result, the negative experiences in your life do not cancel or reduce your value. Those negative experiences add to your value. When you have overcome tough times and challenges, people want to hear the story of how you overcame. History is not made by going through life comfortably. History is made by people who thrived through difficult times. You are only known by the things you overcame.

If you write a book about your tough times, it would be a bestseller. If you write a song about your challenges in a relationship and how you were abused, people will listen. If you mentor others who have gone through what you have been through, people will surely subscribe. People will want to hear from you because they want to know how you overcame it. They want to be inspired by your story. You see how your negative experiences can be a cue to your purpose. God is very intentional concerning anything He allows us to go through. This is why I love the scripture that says, 'And we know that ALL THINGS

WORK TOGETHER FOR GOOD to those who love God, to those who are the called according to His purpose.'[56] God can use even the bad things to work together for your good. You can find purpose in your pain, in your misery, in your challenges, and still, be able to help others through theirs. This is what purpose is about.

From the many studies I have done on the subject of purpose and the many people I have spoken to in my seminars, workshops, and masterclasses, one thing I have found is that it is a great privilege to have been through tough times. Yes! Your story is a great gem if you have been through negative experiences and have overcome it. You are carrying about a goldmine and you don't even know it. The very thing you seem to not be proud of is the source of your value. The very thing that seems to make you weep or put you in trauma, everything you think about it or remember is the very thing God wants to use to heal and set others free.

If you are currently going through a negative experience right now, I want to plead with you not to give up. As weird as this may sound, count it all joy that you are going through it. Many people are going to be inspired by your story in the future and because of those destinies, you cannot afford to give up. You cannot afford to take your own life or go into depression. I write this to give you a new perspective on your pain and misery. Your misery may be a mystery to you right now, but I assure you it will be the source of your miracles very soon. The world will come to hear your story and many will be healed.

---

[56] Romans 8:28

I want to tell you 5 things you must do with your story:

1. You must accept/acknowledge your story

Many people are still denying their stories. They can't believe what happened to them actually happened, or they are simply wishing it didn't happen to them. For people like this, whatever happened to them has made them bitter, and not better. For such people, they never want to be identified by that story, so they try and do all they can to bury it. They don't want any ear to hear it because they keep wishing it never happened.

> *"Until you have accepted, embraced, and taken responsibility for your story, you will never be able to inspire others with it."*

Listen, until you acknowledge your story, you will always live a bitter life. In fact, it is impossible for you to fulfil purpose without acknowledging and accepting your story. God cannot do anything with a story you refuse to accept.

God does not want you to live a bitter life. He wants you to live a better life. So, begin to accept your story. Yes, it happened to you and it happened for a purpose.

2. You must embrace your story

After accepting your story, you must begin to embrace it. I love to say it like this, you must hug your story. You must fall in love with your own story. Even if it's a story of guilt, shame or reproach, you must learn to love it.

You will never be able to fulfil your purpose if you don't embrace your story. Embracing your story will help you to stop playing the victim card. Embracing your story will help you come to terms with the fact that what happened to you does not define you. Embracing your story will help you to become enthusiastic about it.

3. You must take responsibility for your story

To take responsibility for your story means to stop blaming people for it. Maybe you were a victim in your story – for instance, your parents abandoned you or someone molested you – you still have to take responsibility for that story. As long as you keep blaming others for what happened to you, you will always be a victim.

> *"Embracing your story will help you come to terms with the fact that what happened to you does not define you."*

To take responsibility does not mean you have to blame yourself for what happened, it just means you decide you will no longer let it hold you back. It means you're ready to accept it happened, forgive yourself and others, and move on with your life. For your story to turn to glory, you must take responsibility for it.

4. You must Inspire with Your Story

Until you have accepted, embraced, and taken responsibility for your story, you will never be able to inspire others with it. This is because when you tell your story, you will tell it from a place of hurt, pains and unforgiveness. Such story does not inspire people, instead, they will either feel pity, anger, sadness, or sorrow for you.

But when you have accepted, embraced, and taken responsibility for your story, when you tell it, you will tell it from a place of victory, joy, peace, hope, love, forgiveness, and glory. This is what makes people inspired. You will feel like the true champion you are who has been through pain and adversity and conquered. You are a victor not the vanquished, so tell your story from a place of victory and inspire people joyfully.

> *"The very crisis you have been through is your purpose calling out to you."*

5. You Must Profit from Your Story

You should not just stop at inspiring people with your story, you should absolutely profit from it too. Tell it on every stage you find yourself, publish it in a book. A true story of victory that inspires others often become   bestsellers.
See, there are destinies connected to yours story. You must share your story with the world. Yes! You heard me. Now is the time to share your story on a global stage. You have to be that beacon of hope, faith, love, light, and purpose to others. Your purpose is calling out to you. You have been quiet for too long.

The very crisis you have been through is your purpose calling out to you. Now, share your story with the world. Bring hope and healing to others. There are lives and destinies connected to your story. All they are waiting for is to hear it and hear it from you. If you have a gift of writing, now is the time to put it in a book. If you have the gift of speaking, now is the time to begin sharing your stories on any platform you can find. If no one is giving you a platform, for now, create your platform. Use your social media as your platform. I am sure the world cannot wait to hear the story of how you overcame it. I am rooting for you and I believe in you.

D. Look Around

Another place to look is around you, within your community, your environment, your city, for problems that are always calling out to you daily. From Africa to Asia, Europe to Oceania, I have spoken to so many people about their purposes to know this to be true. All of us have those problems we see around us that we complain about, we blame others about, yet every single day when we see those problems, we never stop talking about them. What we do not realise is that those problems around us are calling forth our purposes.

Your problem is that you keep blaming others about the problem, not realising that it is the calling and purpose within you that are beckoning you. I remember the story of the popular Nobel Peace Prize winner, Mother Theresa, the Roman Catholic nun who devoted her life to serving the poor and destitute. Before she was awarded the Nobel Peace Prize for selfless work in 1979, Mother Theresa was a teacher in India, and seeing the poverty in Calcutta especially within her community, she couldn't bear it. She had to do something. She started a mission she called, 'The Missionaries of Charity.'

Her vision was to help the people she saw around her that people were not ready to look after including the government of the country. She chose to live among the poorest of people in Calcutta just to be able to cater to them and devote her life to serving them. She would even dress in the Indian Sari. She wanted to connect with the poorest in her community because of her heart for them. History records that she did that during two major crises including the Bengal famine in 1943 and the Hindu/Muslim clash in 1946 but she did not forget her purpose. It rather spurred her to action.

> *"Your problem is that you keep blaming others for the problem, not realising that it is the calling and purpose within you that are beckoning you."*

She didn't blame the government, the schools, she took it upon herself to address the needs that were calling out to her in her community and she found purpose doing that. In her words, 'Not all of us can do great things, but we can do small things with great love.' Wow! What a heart! So many people have criticised her work and I am not writing this to defend anything she did or did not do, but her heart for the needs in her community cannot go unnoticed. Likewise, when you decide to stop blaming the government for those problems you see around you and get to work and start doing something about it, you will realise that purpose has been calling out to you all the time.

For instance, you have been seeing people who are uneducated in your community and this for some reason angers you or makes you weep, then you must realise that is purpose calling out to you. You don't have to have great resources to get started. Just start with one person at a time. Purpose always starts small, as with anything that eventually becomes great. You have to start somewhere.

Purpose in Crisis | **Samuel Ekundayo**

When I got to New Zealand in 2008, one prevalent thing I kept hearing was the problem of suicide. Whenever I read about the statistics that almost about 2 people die daily to suicide, most of whom are teenagers and youths, I am always distraught. On some days, I find myself weeping for people I do not even know. In my initial years here, I was always blaming the government by asking, 'What is the government doing about this issue?'

One day, I remember asking the same question and complaining to some of my friends. I was even telling them about how it must be because many people do not know God, which means, I know the source of the problem, but I was not doing anything other than complaining. That night, when my friends left for their respective homes, I had an epiphany within me. More like a voice that asked, 'So, what are you going to do about it?' I was challenged within my spirit and I said to myself, 'Enough is enough, I am going to stop blaming people about this problem and I will start doing something about it.' At the time of making that decision, I had no idea what I was going to do.

But that burden would not just let me go. Every single day, I began ruminating about how I could do something about it. One day, in 2017, I got an idea to write for 30 days, inspirational and motivational articles that inspire and encourage people not to commit suicide. I did it in November 2017 to be precise. I had no idea how it would turn out, but I just took that bold step. In hindsight, I realise it was my purpose of making sure people fulfil their potentials and live their purpose that was calling out to me. I am not happy when people die prematurely or are just living aimlessly without fulfilling their purposes. It breaks my heart. Like I said earlier, many times, I weep for these people that I do not even know.

So, I wrote the articles and shared them on all my social media platforms. The campaign went on throughout that month. Before I knew it, I was called to the Parliament in New Zealand to talk about the project. I have appeared on several panels, forums, and platforms speaking about this subject. I was also featured in a news article.[57]

*"It is impossible to answer the call of purpose and your work
will go unnoticed."*

It is impossible to answer the call of purpose and your work will go unnoticed. You may have been sitting on your purpose all these while simply because you have not taken action on the very problem or need that has been constantly calling out to you in your environment, your community, your church, your city, your place of work. Especially when that call is incessant, you should take it seriously; it often connotes you have been equipped to solve or do something about the problem.

I can hear you say, 'Samuel, you don't understand. The problem that is calling out my name in my community is too big for me to solve. It's the problem of the government, not mine.' Listen, have you ever wondered why it appears that amongst your friends, your neighbours, your co-workers, your church members, you seemingly are the only one this particular problem is so vivid to? Have you ever wondered why it

---

[57] Article here: https://www.stuff.co.nz/auckland/local-news/western-leader/99172125/academic-raises-awareness-for-suicide-prevention

appears no one else but you is heavily concerned about it? Have you ever wondered why it appears no one else cares so much about it but you? It's because there is something within you that is calling out to you to solve the problem. And yes, the problem may appear bigger than you. One thing you must realise is you may not be able to solve the entire problem, but there is a role you have been created to play in the solution to that problem.

> *"This problem that appears you are the only one vehemently concerned about is possibly linked to why God created you."*

In chapter one where I described purpose, I talked about how purpose is an assignment and a solution to a particular problem. This problem that appears you are the only one vehemently concerned about is possibly linked to why God created you. God carefully and thoughtfully made every one of us and your existence is proof that there is a problem or a need your life addresses.

Stop ignoring that call, instead start doing something about it. All you need to do is answer the call. You don't need to figure out how and what yet. Just answer the call. The moment it registers and settles in your heart that you have answered the call of purpose and you're no longer complaining about it and you're willing to act, ideas will just start coming to you, resources will start showing up to help you address the need. I have come to realise that the very things you need to start addressing the problem are already within you, all you need to do is answer the call and they will start getting activated. The money you need, the ideas you need, the people you need, will just start coming your way as soon as you decide to do something about it.

That was the case when I decided to answer the call of doing something about suicide in my community – New Zealand. All of a sudden, the idea to write articles came. While writing them, I was introduced to journalists who decided to do a publication about it in the newspaper. I also met with parliament members who asked me to come in to talk about my project. I was introduced to people who gave me their platforms to talk about it, including a radio station. Doors just began opening left, right, and centre; doors I had no idea were there before I answered the call.

One of the people I got introduced to suggested I published the articles as a book and I was like wow! I decided to put them together in a book. Now, the book is published on Amazon titled, *30 Reasons to Stay: Say No to Suicide And Give Life Another Try*[58]

Since publishing the articles into a book (e-book only as at the time of writing this book), I have had the ideas of making hard copies of the book to take to prisons and schools where I can reach more people with my message of hope. Someone wrote a review of the book on Amazon that touched me – *'Life is a struggle for me right now. Last night I had so many thoughts and just NEEDED something positive. Somehow I came across this book in my kindle app. I wasn't even LOOKING. I read every word and cried. Cried for myself and cried over feeling like you as a writer, could see into my soul last night. So thank you. Just. Thank you'*

---

[58] Get the book here: https://www.amazon.com/30-Reasons-Stay-Suicide-Another-ebook/dp/B07TML9V1Y

Just imagine if I failed to answer that call. Now, I want you to imagine the problems and needs in your community, your city, your school, your workplace, that have been calling out to you but you have been ignoring and have been blaming others but yourself. Imagine the lives that are perishing because of your stubbornness. Imagine lives that could be suffering more than they should because of your indignance instead of you doing something about it. All you need to get started is within you.

For instance, maybe you have been noticing the group of youths in your community who seem to have no vision for their lives, and the fact that their lives appear to be wasting away gets you angry or makes you sad, that could be purpose calling out to you. Maybe for you, it is the women who have been abused that seem to always be the problem in your community that makes you angry or sad; could it be that purpose has been calling out to you all these while and you have been ignoring it? Perhaps there are orphans in your city that you know their story and how life has become miserable for them because they have been abandoned and you see them every day and deep within, you are angry and sad at the same time; could it be that purpose has been calling out to you?

What I would like you to do is take a seat, grab a pen and paper and try to identify the patterns of the problems and needs in your community and environment that always seem to call out to you, that appears you are the only one that notices or the seemingly most concerned in your neighbourhood. List them and try to identify the pattern and you would notice something strange – they are linked to something you could do something about. Your purpose has been calling out to you all the while. You need to take responsibility and stop blaming others. Acknowledge and accept the call and the ideas you need to be a solution to the problem or address the needs will begin to flow. You can do it!

> *"Some experiences you have had in times past, however old, can add value to your discovery and pursuit of purpose."*

E. Look Back

I know you have been told by many preachers, motivational speakers, and people who mean you well never to look back because there is nothing in your past that you need. I agree with them, but I dare say that one of the places to get cues to your purpose is your past. Yes, the past is one of the places to look.

Some experiences you have had in times past, however old, can add value to your discovery and pursuit of purpose. See, nothing just happens! Most of the experiences of your past have a link to your purpose and your identity. Like we discussed in the *look down* section, they may be unpalatable but their negativity does not change their value to your purpose and destiny. I mean even the most challenging childhood can be significant to the discovery of your purpose. All you need is to look at the experiences from a different perspective.

One key question that can bring this cue to fore is: *'When have I felt most fulfilled in my life so far?'* No doubt, this question will cause you to cast your mind back on your life, but that is the goal. For me, I am most fulfilled when I speak and people's lives are impacted and transformed. I noticed that whenever I am invited to share what I know about the

Purpose in Crisis | **Samuel Ekundayo**

topics that I am passionate about, or when I write and people thank me for providing them with a fresh perspective to life and helping them move forward in an area of life, I always felt like jumping off and raising the roof. The common pattern for me is the desire to just help people move forward with their lives. This was how I knew that I am a motivational/transformational speaker and writer. I have since devoted my life to this calling and purpose. If you ask yourself the same questions, you will likely pick on a few experiences of your past that have brought you a sense of fulfilment, and you can then look at the common pattern and you may be able to get a cue to your purpose.

I went to speak in Tasmania Australia and a lady came to see me after because she was puzzled about her purpose in life. I asked her to share with me her story and she began to tell me how she enjoyed cooking so much and how she cooked almost every day and delights so much in just cooking for people freely. She would cook and take it to church and back home in Africa, she had a restaurant and for her, that was when she felt fulfilled. She said these words, 'Dr. Sam, I feel fulfilled whenever I am cooking.' I said to her, 'No doubt, this is a cue to your purpose and calling.' Let me highlight here that before she came to me, she had been told by many people not to ever think of cooking as a career because no one makes a living out of cooking as a migrant in Australia. She had been fed this lie and for economic and financial reasons, she had been advised to go study nursing. I was glad I was able to help her shed some light on the common patterns in her experiences of the times she had felt fulfilled to see that cooking has a major role to play in her fulfilment in life.

110

Beyond this question, your childhood experience also matters. Let's take a look:

Magical Moments in Childhood

Nick Craig, in his book, *Leading from Purpose,* wrote a chapter on magical childhood moments. He emphasised that 'If purpose is the unique gift we bring to the world, the curious child inside us probably knows where it is hidden. Our childhood is full of moments in which we were totally at peace with the world and ourselves, or completely in the flow of being ourselves and doing what we loved and were good at.'[59] You would agree with me that there are several childhood memories we just never forget. They keep playing in our heads since then and recalling them tends to kick into epic mental and emotional space. Yes, childhood memories can be very fresh and vibrant like something that happened yesterday. In the words of Nick, 'When we evoke strong and powerful childhood memories in ourselves, we re-experience the moments of wonder and insight that are the basic ingredients of purpose.' I agree.

I am reminded of my childhood days. My parents were fond of only playing gospel VHS in our home. While other kids were consuming things like cartoons, action movies, and comedies, we were always watching one preacher or the other. In my early formative years from the age of five, I recall watching Evangelist Robert W. Schambach, Evangelist Reinhard Bonnke, both of blessed memories, Kenneth Copeland, Bishop TD Jakes, and so on. We had their VHS in our

---

[59] Leading from Purpose by Nick Craig | pg 35

house. As I watched these men of God preach, there was always a stirring on my inside. I remember saying to my parents that I wanted to be an Evangelist and do all I saw Evangelist Reinhard Bonnke doing on TV, preaching, praying for people, and getting lives saved. I was so passionate that by the time I completed my Primary School and was interviewed for my choice of High School back then in the Northern States of Nigeria, they asked me which school I wanted as my first choice and I replied, 'Missionary School, please.' My interviewer was shocked as there were no Missionary Schools owned by the government in that part of Nigeria. He asked for my second choice and I said the same thing. The man was so confused he wrote nothing down for both my first and second choice on paper. My parents found out about this when the list of students who had been posted to schools emerged and my name was not found on any of the lists. They decided to investigate further, only to find out my interviewer did not write anything down for my choice of school. It wasn't his fault, I was consumed by purpose and there were no government-owned missionary schools in the city.

Also, my dad was fond of buying and reading books. I remember on my eighth birthday, my dad bought me a book titled, I saw Heaven, by Roberts Liardon. I remember him saying these exact words, 'If he saw heaven at eight, you too can.' I went on to read the book and I was so inspired that I would pray daily to see heaven the way Roberts Liardon did. That inspiration lasted for years and I began to read more books by him. Also, my dad is a preacher and at that age, I saw him preach a lot on the pulpit, and his life as a preacher inspired me. I wanted to be on the pulpit too someday. I remember there was a day we went out to preach in our neighbourhood and we met a man who we were trying to convince to accept Jesus into his life and while my parents were talking to him, (I can't particularly recall how the conversation was going that day now) I remember very vividly that I added my words and quoted a scripture from the Bible I would never forget. I said to him, 'Sir for by grace are ye saved through faith; and that not of yourselves: it is the gift of God: Not of works, lest any man should boast.' [60] I am not sure I even understood the full meaning of the scripture but it must have been one of the memory verses my parents taught me at the age, but it appeared to make so much sense to whatever they were talking about because they all paused, looked at me, and the man looked impressed and not only that, he was in church that weekend and gave his life to Christ. My point is, if you can cast your mind back to your past, you are likely to be able to epitomise your purpose in a way that makes uncommon sense to you.

F. Look Forward

Another place to look for cues to our purpose is in the future. For some of us, for most of our lives, we have had this vision of the future, a longing, and belonging that we may not be able to explain how we came about, but just won't go away! For some people, it is the dream of an 'ideal life' that they've held within themselves for years. More like, 'If life was perfect, I would be travelling all over the world speaking to thousands of people every single day.' The future is a vision of your highest self that you have held in your mind for a long time but for various reasons including your financial status, lack of encouragement from friends and family, ignorance of how to navigate such a dream,

---

[60] Ephesians 2:8-9

you have parked it. That 'dream' might just be a cue to your gift and purpose. For instance, for me, it was becoming a professor. While I had no idea why I wanted to become a professor, from the age of 14, the image of my ideal self was clear. I always saw myself imparting knowledge to so many people. Whenever I closed my eyes to think about my future, I never fail to get that image of me teaching students in a classroom setting. Interestingly, whenever this imagination comes, I would not see myself teaching kids, they were always adults in my class, so I knew it's something of the higher institution. No doubt, this was a cue to my purpose as I am now, through my speaking, teachings, workshops, coaching, helping people discover their purposes so they can maximise their potentials. Apart from the dream to be a professor, the vision of my 'highest self' is travelling the world speaking to millions, and writing books published in several languages of the world. This vision has consumed me so much that I confess it to myself every morning with so much passion. That vision is a cue that I was born with a message to the world. This reminds me of the story of Joseph in the Bible[61], he had the vision/dream of his highest self as a young man. More than once, he saw himself or representation of himself being honoured and bowed down to by his brothers and parents. When he dared to share the dream with his brothers, they hated him. But that vision was the pull to his future. Even his father could not understand. His father asked him to keep quiet. Likewise, you may have this vision of your highest self for a long time. Your long term dreams, visions, and imaginations are cues to your purpose. Let me ask you: What is the vision of your highest self that you have conceived within you for a

---

[61] Genesis 37

while now that you are either afraid to share with someone or maybe you have shared and you have been discouraged?

SOME PARTING WORDS

If you have managed to complete this book, I'd like to congratulate you. Please don't just see the completion of the book as an end, see it as a means to an end. See it as a call to awaken the leader in you.

I want to believe my stories and the principles shared have helped you position yourself rightly to be victorious through every crisis situation of your life.

I believe your time has come to live with faith, strength and courage, through every storm and boisterous winds of life to take your place, rule and dominate as you have been called, mandated and blessed to.

I believe in you.

- Dr Samuel Ekundayo
The Purpose Preacher

ABOUT THE AUTHOR

Dr. Samuel Ekundayo is a Senior Lecturer, author, preacher, and transformational speaker. Often referred to as 'The Purpose Preacher', his mandate is to help people discover their purpose so they can maximise their potentials towards a fulfilled, influential, and impactful life to the glory of God.

As an internationally sought-after speaker, he has been privileged to consult for corporate organisations, as well as speak on various platforms including churches, independently organised conferences, and events all over the world.

In 2019, he gave a TEDx Talk on 'Purpose, the ultimate cure to suicide', an inspirational talk that has changed lives and helped many discover their life's purpose.

He is also the founder of *Motivitality*, a weekly motivational video series on social media with the vision of helping men and women find their purpose and maximise their potentials, with over 20,000 fans and over 200,000 views.

He has authored three other books – Arise and Succeed: Becoming the Champion you are, FIRED UP: The ultimate guide to focus and consistency in every endeavour, and 30 Reasons to Stay: Say no to suicide and give life another try – all of which can be found in major bookstores online.

He is married to a woman he calls his Treasure – Blessing Ekundayo – and they are blessed with two boys, to the glory of God.

You can find more about him on his website – *SamuelEkundayo.com*